MW01702125

PRAISE FOR *CREATIVE ZING!* FROM CREATIVE LEADERS

***"Sam's fire-starting ideas will resonate when you hear them and work like gangbusters when you apply them.** I cannot recommend a more eye-opening guidebook for someone starting out on their way to a meaningful creative life or someone who wants to find their way back to one."*

BRIAN COLLINS, Chief Creative Officer, COLLINS, design consultancy firm

***"If you're getting ready to pitch your best solutions, but feel a little hesitant, fearful, or unsure, then you will absolutely love Sam's book.** The inspiration in these pages is like a personal pep talk* from *the master of pitching ideas."*

ANDY BRENITS, president of inSource, the association for in-house creative leadership

***"Sam Harrison steers us off the bland, safe, boring path**— equipping us with bite-size tips and micro-actions to add more creative zing to our lives."*

LISA MAULHARDT, Chief Marketing Officer, SYPartners, management and design consultancy firm

MORE PRAISE FOR *CREATIVE ZING!* FROM CREATIVE LEADERS

*"**I'm better because of this book. I don't know how anyone who reads it wouldn't be.** Every topic is short and digestible in minutes if not seconds. Each features real-life stories as connective threads. Sam provides sound counsel and also translates it into applicable action."*

STEFAN MUMAW, author of *Creative Boot Camp* and Creative Director at First Person, a digital agency

*"Having worked at, consulted with and trained in-house agency teams, I know how a creative person can feel at a loss for new ideas. **This book offers real-world tactical advice and activities to jolt us into the creative action** of not only coming up with ideas, but also how to make them real and sell them with passion and commitment."*

ANDY EPSTEIN, author of *The Corporate Creative* and Director of Solutions at Cella Consulting

*"**If you are looking to unlock more creativity and share it more successfully, this book is for you!** Sam does a masterful job of meeting you where you are and giving you actionable guidance to implement in your creative process—whether you are early in your career or a seasoned veteran."*

JUSTIN AHRENS, author of *Life Kerning* and Creative Director at Rule29 Creative Agency

CREATIVE ZING

SPARK YOUR CREATIVITY & POWERFULLY PRESENT YOUR IDEAS

SAM HARRISON

CREATIVE ZING! Spark Your Creativity and Powerfully Present Your Ideas

Cover Design: Ian Koviak

Interior Design: Ian Koviak and Alan Hebel

Copyeditor: Kim Bookless

Printed in the United States

ISBN: 978-1-733-44390-6

For information or permissions, write to author at:

Box 1632,Chattahoochee Hills, GA 30268

ALSO BY SAM HARRISON

Zing!

5 steps & 101 tips for creativity on command

IdeaSpotting

How to find your next great idea

IdeaSelling

Successfully pitch your creative ideas to bosses, clients and other decision makers

SAM HARRISON is a speaker, writer and coach on creativity topics and on presentation skills.

www.zingzone.com

CREATIVE

>>>

THE MANIFESTATION OF CREATIVITY, IN OUTPUT AND EXPRESSION, AND A LIFE LIVED WITH PASSION, DISCOVERY AND GENEROSITY.

HOW TO USE THIS BOOK

SINGLE-PAGE MESSAGES. Content is presented as one-page messages. This bite-size format makes insights and suggestions more convenient and digestible for on-the-go creative people who are constantly juggling projects and bombarded with endless information.

THIS BOOK IS A BUFFET. Go straight down the line, reading cover-to-cover and gobbling up everything in sight. Or head directly to morsels that suit your needs. And keep the book handy for future reference when generating ideas or preparing for presentations. ***Creative Zing!*** works in many ways.

With this easy-to-use handbook, **you don't have to sift through hundreds of pages of blather to find help.** Suggestions and insights are right before your eyes. No pretense. No fluff. No fooling. Just lots of Creative Zing!

SIDENOTES. Interspersed throughout this book are sidenote pages with stimulating quotes or quick actions. Use these to inspire your thinking and add extra zing to your creativity.

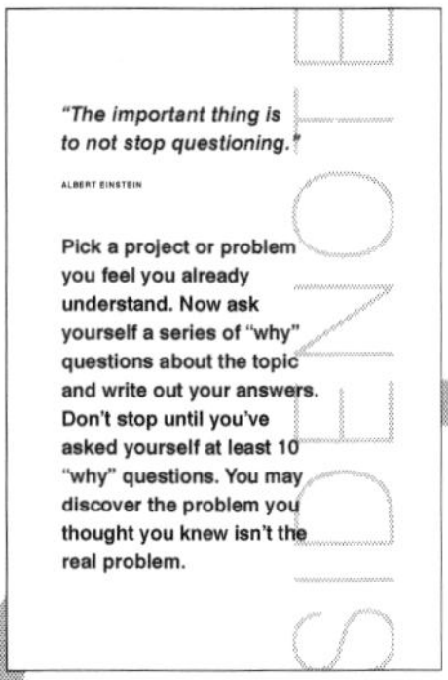

"The important thing is to not stop questioning."

ALBERT EINSTEIN

Pick a project or problem you feel you already understand. Now ask yourself a series of "why" questions about the topic and write out your answers. Don't stop until you've asked yourself at least 10 "why" questions. You may discover the problem you thought you knew isn't the real problem.

SIDENOTE

YOU CAN ONLY HAVE A LIMITED NUMBER OF IDEAS IN YOUR LIFETIME.

That's not true. I just made it up.

But you've probably had times when you felt this statement was absolutely true, that you had run out of ideas, that your creativity was extinct. Gone. Kaput.

I've certainly had such moments. But, truth is, **creativity is always available to us, despite those times when we convince ourselves it's long gone.**

Creativity is innate in humans. We arrive in this world as highly creative beings (for evidence, spend time with kindergarten kids). **Creativity has always been there. We just need to cultivate that creativity throughout our lives.**

But that's not always easy. **Systems are in place to discourage creativity.** Teachers say don't ask questions. Parents say don't be silly. Bosses say don't make mistakes. Society says don't be different. Negative voices say no way.

So to stay creative, we have to practice creative habits. And that's the purpose of this book. **It's all about creative performance**. Here you'll find suggestions and examples to fill your life with ***Creative Zing!***

ZOOM INTO CREATIVE ZINGING!

As I see it, each of us is always in one of three zones—Zombie Zone, Zigzag Zone or, when on target, **Creative Zing Zone**.

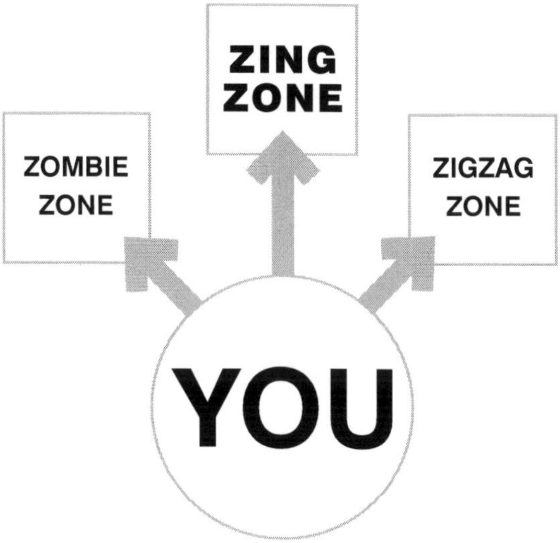

In the Zombie Zone, you're sluggish and bored, maybe a bit comatose. You're likely stuck in a comfort zone or velvet rut, doing the same old things in the same old ways. And you're consequently coming up with the same old ideas.

In the Zigzag Zone, you're spinning in circles or yo-yoing up and down. Creativity is rarely linear, but in this mode, chaos reigns supreme. No focus or direction, process or plan. Motion is mistaken for action.

In the Creative Zing Zone, things start looking up. Your creativity hits on all cylinders. You're filled with passion and punch, vitality and velocity. You enthusiastically crank out fresh ideas. And when you present those ideas, people understand and embrace them.

Creative Zing! helps when you need ideas and when you need to convey those ideas to others.

While there is no cookie-cutter formula for creativity, there are ways highly creative people often move toward powerful ideas. This is especially true for those having to come up with ideas on a deadline—designers, marketers, product developers, event planners, advertising and PR folks, freelancers, architects, teachers, columnists and scores of others.

When ideas aren't coming your way—or when you have ideas that don't see the light of day—***Creative Zing!* comes to the rescue with five factors: Explore, Experiment, Exhale, Examine and Express.**

TAKE A LOOK >

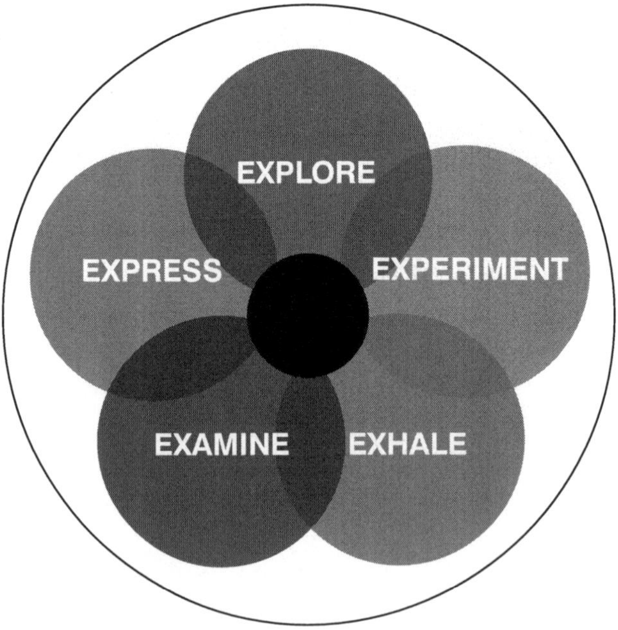

CREATIVE

THE HEART OF

ZING

EXPLORE **pages 13-55**

Deep dig to uncover evidence and insights leading to ideas. Go past the obvious to the original. Leap beyond ordinary to extraordinary.

EXPERIMENT **pages 57-101**

Open windows and let air rush in. No judging or opinions. Cuts come later. For now, it's quantity, not quality.

EXHALE **pages 103-114**

Come up for air. Pause. Let go. Get away. Leave room for a new perspective and allow the subconscious to do its thing.

EXAMINE **pages 115-137**

Review and probe ideas. Iterate and dilate. Select the very best.

EXPRESS **pages 139-227**

Apply strong presenting and selling skills. Convey how ideas look in the real world—now and in the future. Make decision makers hungry for your ideas.

OK, enough small talk.
Let's start moving
toward your

~~ZOMBIE ZONE~~

~~ZIGZAG ZONE~~

CREATIVE ZING ZONE

RIGHT NOW

"Whatever inspiration is, it's born from a continuous 'I don't know.'"

WISTAWA SZYMBORSKA, POET & NOBEL PRIZE WINNER

EXPLORE

"Everything is raw material. Everything is relevant. Everything is usable. Everything feeds my creativity. But without proper preparation, I cannot see it, retain it and use it."

TWYLA THARP, CHOREOGRAPHER

TIPS TO BOOST CREATIVITY

Creativity is a natural resource. It comes as standard equipment with being human. But creativity becomes dull and nonresponsive without care and feeding.

The next time you or your team slide into that Zombie Zone of bland ideas and demoralizing ruts, audit your habits and practices.

For starters, are you staying curious? Because curiosity is straight fire for creativity. By exploring, you bring insights and inspiration to imagination.

"People who are curious will develop themselves," Mark Templeton, Citrix former CEO, told *The New York Times*. "They'll discover things, they'll invent things."

ACTION

Train yourself to stop, look and listen—at work, at home or when out and about. Be mindful of people, places and things. Act as if your eyes are a camera and your ears a microphone, capturing what you see and hear around you. Take notes!

On following pages are four more quick boosts for creativity >

Boost Creativity: Be Playful

As a speaker and writer, I often visit the workplaces of clients, associates and friends. Walking down hallways, I can usually tell if creativity is flourishing. In highly creative organizations, there's scattered laughter. Spirited conversation. Some messiness. There's whimsical artwork here and there. In short, there's a detectable attitude of play blended with business.

Maintaining creativity requires a bit of childlike behavior—not childish but childlike. We have to shed some inhibitions. Ask simple questions. Dwell in daydreams. Laugh at ourselves.

Of course, playful practices don't always come easily. Such behavior has sometimes been coached, taught or managed right out of us, perhaps when we were kids. As early as grade school, children are told to stop being silly, stop asking questions, stop daydreaming.

ACTION

Add play to your day. Take work seriously but don't take yourself too seriously. Shake off useless inhibitions. Laugh with team members. Ask simple questions. Roam out of bounds when generating ideas. And make sure your workspace has visual touches of playfulness.

Boost Creativity: Be Generous

Creativity is a team sport. Our creative resources come alive as we share insights and ideas.

Be willing to share your ideas—and also be available to receive ideas from team members, friends and family. A fastball pitcher can't be successful without someone to catch his pitches. Likewise with ideas—for every idea thrown out, there needs to be a catcher who carefully listens and withholds instant judgment.

ACTION

Help establish an atmosphere of generosity in your workplace. Freely give ideas. Attentively listen to ideas of others. Celebrate and support creativity. And develop a personal network for sharing books, websites, blogs, videos, films and other creative stimulation.

Boost Creativity: Be Courageous

Being creative isn't for sissies. It takes courage to present ideas for the world to critique and possibly reject. But payoffs outweigh risks.

Steve Jobs displayed the bravery needed for innovation. He was a "genius combination of talent, vision and guts," according to Paola Antonelli, curator at the Museum of Modern Art. His vision and talent allowed him to imagine revolutionary advances in technology—but without his bold courage, Apple would never have become an innovative powerhouse.

ACTION

Have you held back on discussing and developing ideas because you fear criticism or ridicule? Review those ideas to determine if they possess novelty and value. If so, muster the courage to bring the ideas forward, regardless of pessimists and cynics.

Boost Creativity: Be Persistent

Having the seed of an idea only starts the creative process. Reaching the finish line takes time and energy. Starts and stops. Thought and action. Presentations and negotiations.

Many great ideas are at this very moment gathering dust in boxes and drawers. Simply because their owners didn't stick it out.

ACTION

Check for ideas you've stashed away because of criticism or rejection. Ask yourself if extra effort might bring them to reality. If so, surge ahead!

"Never let your dreams hide behind the door of opportunity."

—DEBASISH MRIDHA, NEUROLOGIST AND PHILOSOPHER

CURIOSITY OPENS DOORS

Curiosity is always the first trait detected in highly creative people. Cats have nothing on creative folks when it comes to being curious.

"My favorite words are possibilities, opportunities and curiosity," said photographer Mario Testino. "I think if you are curious, you create opportunities, and then if you open the doors, you create possibilities."

Walt Disney also associated curiosity with open doors. "We keep moving forward, opening new doors and doing new things," he said, "because we're curious and curiosity keeps leading us down new paths."

Read on to learn three ways curiosity opens doors >

Curiosity Inspires Creative Living

Curiosity lifts us out of humdrum routines and moves us into uncharted territory. Life becomes more exciting and energetic, creative and rewarding.

"The work I did is the work I know, and the work I do is the work I don't know," composer Philip Glass told *The New York Times*. "And it's the not knowing that makes it interesting."

ACTION

Is what you know stopping you from looking at what you don't know? Get curious about topics outside your scope of knowledge and daily routines.

I WANT TO LEARN MORE ABOUT

Curiosity Looks Ahead

If you are curious about people—asking more and more questions—you can see beyond today. With relentless curiosity and questioning, your ideas will meet wants and needs, both now and in the future.

My friend Brian Collins, founder of COLLINS brand experience design, points out that seeking and anticipating allow you to reframe problems. "Enough with 'problem *solving*,'" says, Collins. "Start with 'problem *seeking*.' Seeking is leading. It uses a combination of aggressive curiosity, loads of imagination and empathy. And it leverages deep and broad background.

"Always ask the next question. And then ask the question after that. And so on. You'll soon find answers to important questions that people don't know how to ask."

ACTION

Be curious about customers, peers, suppliers, friends, family and strangers. What makes them laugh and cry? Complain and praise? Shout and scream? Learn their fears and concerns, hopes and dreams. Let questioning and observing reveal how the future might look and feel for clients and customers.

Curiosity Finds Answers

By being curious about other businesses and professions, we can sometimes borrow from their solutions.

For example, a product designer at Mattson, a food development firm, was looking for a way to add more sweetness and citrus flavor to a low-calorie strawberry cookie.

Curiosity led her to sample low-fat cheese tortilla chips. She quickly realized that cheese powder on the outside of the chips intensified their flavor. So she dusted her test cookies with sugar, citric acid and strawberry flavor, and, eureka!—tangy, sweeter low-fat cookies.

Borrowing can be the basis for new ideas. It's not where you take it from, it's where you take it to.

ACTION

Be curious about the practices and solutions of others. They may hold the answers to your problems.

GATHER STRING

"Gathering string" is jargon used by media reporters to describe the process of seeking out facts, quotes and other tidbits for stories.

That "string" might be an intriguing photo on a wall, nervous twitch on a face or glib post on Facebook.

Similarly, you can gather string to aid creativity. Information scientists call this "super encountering"—using eyes and ears to lead you to clues.

If we always look in the same old places for the same old things, we'll always have the same old ideas. Instead, have super encounters and rendezvous with the unfamiliar. Gather string for your next great idea.

Look around right now. Quickly write down five objects or details you haven't noticed today:

Soak in your surroundings to ignite creativity.

WE CAN SEE AND STILL BE BLIND

The Blind Boys of Alabama is an acclaimed gospel group that has won five Grammys, performed for three White Houses and delighted audiences around the world.

In an NPR interview, Ricky McKinnie, a singer and drummer for the group, said this about his lack of sight: "I can't see, but I'm not blind."

He makes it clear that he's not blind to the feelings of his audience. Not blind to the actions of people. Not blind to life.

That's a powerful message, because many people have 20/20 vision yet are blind to the world around them.

I'm sometimes guilty. How about you? Are you sometimes blind to surroundings in a restaurant, shop or airport? Blind to what's happening on streets when heading home? Blind to goings-on in workplace or marketplace?

Be aware. Pay attention. Feel the fine details. Creativity isn't blind.

"Rigor leads to rigor mortis."

DEBORAH KASS, ARTIST

Five ways I'll break out of routines:

____

____

____

____

____

LOOSEN LIGAMENTS OF CRAMPED MINDS

Little questions sometimes solve big problems. Because questions loosen ligaments of cramped minds. Spirited inquiry releases us from trying to solve problems with the same thinking that caused the problems.

So why do we resist asking questions? It's an adult thing. Research shows that asking questions peaks around age five and then steadily drops off, according to Warren Berger, author of *A More Beautiful Question*.

"Some people worry that asking questions at work reveals ignorance," says Berger, "or may be seen as slowing things down."

I say let's slow down. Play dumb. Ask questions. Ask customers questions. Ask bosses questions. Ask team members questions. Ask friends questions. Ask family questions. Ask yourself questions.

Because creative solutions come from having our questions answered and our answers questioned.

“The important thing is to not stop questioning.”

ALBERT EINSTEIN

Pick a project or problem you feel you already understand. Now ask yourself a series of “why” questions about the topic and write out your answers. Don’t stop until you’ve asked yourself at least 10 “why” questions. You may discover the problem you thought you knew isn’t the real problem.

QUESTIONS TO ASK YOURSELF

In the quest for abundant creativity, we ask questions of others—but it's also useful to question ourselves from time to time. Because what's happening in our minds and lives determines whether we're in a Zombie Zone, Zigzag Zone or Creative Zing Zone.

Start by asking yourself this question:

Am I Inspired Or Tired?

Periodically review personal interests and habits—blogs, websites, films, TV shows, restaurants, shops, sports and so on. For each, ask yourself: "Does this tire me or inspire me?" If it inspires you, keep it up. But if it tires you, advance to a fresh source of inspiration.

"I had a habit of reading *The Wall Street Journal* business and tech sections early each morning, thinking the exercise would provide references for my clients," says Lisa Maulhardt, a principle at SYPartners. "But when I found myself dreading the process, I switched to reading a few pages from either a humanities text or literary journal. The change has reawakened my vocabulary and broadened my perspective."

On following pages are three more questions to renew creativity >

What Should I Avoid?

Knowing what we don't want to do helps us look beyond the obvious.

"I want to avoid thinking I already know the answers," says design strategist Lindsey Mosby. "Knowing what to avoid helps me get orthogonal and make mash-ups."

Before heading in any direction, ask yourself: *Is this the best use of my time? Will this point me toward fresh solutions? Or will this direction just steer me toward more of the same old stuff?*

THREE THINGS TO AVOID WHEN EXPLORING:

Always Right Or Always Creative?

Stand tall for your valuable opinions and ideas. But be sagacious and strategic. Because if you're eternally sensitive and relentlessly defensive, you'll eventually become that bitter curmudgeon curled in the corner.

An inability to accept criticism or consider compromises inhibits collaboration and steals time from more creative pursuits.

"Anyone too protective of their ideas is suspect at our firm," says SYPartners' Lisa Maulhardt. "It feels like they're more interested in seeing their imprint than being part of creating the greatest idea possible."

It's one thing to state your case and take pride in your work. It's another to never give an inch and turn every discussion into a debate.

Know when to hold and when to fold.

Can I Fix This?

Dave Werner, senior experience designer for Adobe Character Animator, tells how fixing a mistake led to a more creative solution:

"While working on a *Sesame Street* tribute video, I had someone design calligraphy for the lyrics," says Werner. "But I failed to provide him with the entire song, so he only delivered calligraphy for half of the verses.

"We were up against deadline, so to fix my mistake, I hurriedly scanned colorful magnetic letters and used them for the remainder of the song. This quick fix actually added visual diversity to the final product."

Not fixing mistakes can lead to calamities. But, as Werner's example demonstrates, repairing mistakes can often result in happy outcomes.

Rather than fretting over a mistake, ask yourself: *How can I fix this?*

SIDENOTE

"I think creativity stems from trying to find answers . . . So I think if one has a strong curiosity, one will naturally be creative for life."

GARTH STEIN, AUTHOR

ONE SMALL STEP

When passionate about a creative project, it's tempting to tackle too much at once, resulting in frustration, anxiety and, in some cases, defeat.

Instead, break down projects into bite-size pieces and ask: *What's the next small step I need to take?*

Begin by examining the big picture, making sure you know how the end should look. Then probe the parts, determining a logical order based on urgency, importance and what steps have to happen for the next steps to happen. Establish plans and timelines.

"I try to see the big picture, but manage the little parts," says design strategist Lindsey Mosby. "We need to be bold enough to look at the big picture, then decide what can be done sooner, easier and simpler."

CHECK YOUR POSITION

In an episode of Netflix's *Chef Table*, Spanish chef Albert Adria instructs his staff to "always work from the position that you serve the client."

He's referring to positioning of food on plates, of course, but he is also considering how his customers will view, taste and enjoy their dining experience.

Try applying Adria's advice to creativity. When generating ideas, if you work from the position that you serve the client, you'll see through their eyes to better understand present and future needs—and seek solutions that serve them.

It's not about our needs. It's about their needs. It's not about our position. It's about their position.

It's not about how we can be successful. It's about how we can be useful.

KNOW HOW OTHERS SEE THE WORLD

Our ideas can't satisfy customers if we don't know what brings them satisfaction. We must relentlessly strive to understand tastes and preferences, opinions and perceptions.

And these perceptions can vary. For example, vacuum cleaners sold in the United States are usually rather noisy. Because, when it comes to machinery, Americans often associate loud noise with power. European and Asian vacuums tend to be quieter.

Lots of ideas never reach reality simply because they are aliens in the worlds of clients and customers.

Dive into the world of your customers and audiences. Observe them living their lives. What choices do they make? What are they attracted to? What do they avoid? Hear what's being said—but also perceive what isn't being said. Read between the lines. Gather evidence about their world.

SIDENOTE

"The person best qualified to run the experiment is the person nearest to the customer . . . We teach our employees to go and see for themselves what is actually happening in the world."

ERIC RIES, AUTHOR, *The Lean Startup*

BEATING BOREDOM AT WORK

When a project doesn't excite us, it's easy to feel bored and emotionally trapped.

Snap out of boredom by being curious. Because boredom is often simply a loss of curiosity, says Steve Gordon, director of RDQLUS Creative Arts and Marketing.

"If I catch myself bored with a project, I'll stop to read magazines or watch a film, even in the middle of the day," says Gordon. "I search for something far away from work yet linked to the same battery crucial to that work."

And put yourself in the shoes of those who will benefit from the project. What engages them? What excites them? What makes them happy, sad or frustrated?

Curiosity keeps us invigorated by keeping us engaged.

On following pages are four more ways to beat boredom >

Beat Boredom: Laugh

Laughter and boredom can't coexist. So make yourself laugh.

"If I'm bored with a project, I'll pause for a few minutes and watch a couple of YouTube classics," says Julie Klappas, executive creative director at Clementine Entertainment. "Something like 'Girl Licks Pickle,' 'Fat Cat Watches TV' or "Dog Eating Spaghetti' will get me laughing and help brush away boredom."

Dan Monroe, principal and chief wordsmith at Cayenne Creative, turns to his office's vintage shuffleboard table when bored with a project. "Spending a few minutes sliding those metal pucks down the table makes me feel like Mozart with billiard balls in *Amadeus*," he says. "Pretty soon I've conquered my malaise."

What relaxes you and makes you laugh? Turn in that direction the next time you face boredom.

Beat Boredom: Be A Beginner

If you're tired of looking at a project, act as if you're seeing it for the first time.

IDEO's Tom Kelly finds value in adopting beginner's eyes when facing a project he has seen time and again. Speaking at the Creativity World Forum, Kelly reversed "déjà vu," proposing the term "vuja de"—the technique of looking at something you've seen before but seeing it in fresh and novel ways.

Try looking at your project with new eyes. Pretend you're seeing it as a film director, theme park designer or your Aunt Josie—anything that provides a change in perspective.

To beat boredom, make the familiar unfamiliar.

Beat Boredom: Step Out

When a project bores me to a dead stop, I'll grab my laptop and move to another room or nearby coffee shop. A change of venue usually reignites brain cells.

Or maybe just get up and go for a walk, suggests Stephanie Jolluck, creative director of Coleccion Luna and winner of a Spanx Female Entrepreneur Award. "If I'm stuck in boredom, I head outside," she says. "Rain or shine, the outdoors always provides new energy and a fresh perspective."

And try walking in unusual places. "I take walks in hidden suburban neighborhoods, department stores, community colleges," Victor Hwang, vice president of entrepreneurship at Kauffman Foundation, told *The Wall Street Journal*. "When you're walking with no purpose but walking, you see things in a fresh way."

Get up and get going. Abandon boredom.

Beat Boredom:
Stick It Out

Sometimes there's just no quick fix for boredom. When that's the case, suck it up and keep going. Sooner or later, something of interest will show up.

The composer John Cage often cited a Zen koan: "If something is boring after two minutes, try it for four. If still boring, then eight. Then sixteen. Then thirty-two. Eventually one discovers that it is not boring at all."

Boredom is a state of mind. Keep traveling until you enter another state.

"Boredom always precedes a period of great creativity."
Robert M. Pirsig, writer and philosopher

SIDENOTE

Grab pen and paper. Set your phone's alarm for three minutes. Spend those minutes rapidly filling the page with words and images—anything that pops into your head. Don't lift pen from paper. Don't stop. When three minutes are up, ponder the results. Search for patterns. Connect with a project you're working on. Or cluster to generate fresh ideas.

BE CREATIVE WAITING IN LINE

We all spend time waiting in lines—at markets, airports, entertainment venues—but waiting doesn't have to be a waste of time. Rather, turn those waits into wells of creative inspiration. For example:

Reflect While Waiting

Rather than stew, surrender to the queue. Avoid tensing up or reaching for your phone. Instead, let go. Breathe. Let your mind wander and wonder.

"It's important that, even if you don't have balance in your life, you have some time for reflection," Eric Schmidt, past executive chairman of Google, told an interviewer. "The creative parts of one's mind are not on schedule."

Try relaxing with a 4-7-8 breathing exercise advocated by Dr. Andrew Weil: Inhale through your nose for a count of four. Hold your breath for a count of seven. Exhale through your mouth for a count of eight. Repeat four times.

Coming up are two other ways to seek inspiration while stuck waiting >

Study People While Waiting

Most of us classify ourselves as people watchers—after all, our fellow creatures are endlessly entertaining. So while you're waiting around and watching people, search for cues that will guide you to ideas.

Kleenex was first introduced as a remover for cold cream. Only when Kimberly-Clark employees started noticing folks wiping their noses with the tissues did the company market the product as a disposable handkerchief.

Act as if your eyes are a camera and mentally capture the actions, mannerisms and interactions of people. What problem do you detect that you could solve with ideas? What are people doing that might be fodder for a project?

Talk To Yourself While Waiting

Not aloud, or security might escort you out. But as you wait in lines, silently talk with yourself about your projects and problems, stories and solutions.

"Nowadays, we're on our iPhones all the time, and you don't have time to talk with yourself, to analyze," Daniel Lubetzky, CEO of Kind Snacks, told *The New York Times*. "It's hard to figure out things if you are not connecting with yourself and taking the time to be introspective."

Think about a project or situation and ask yourself a series of why, how or what-if questions. Keep digging deeper until you see things from a fresh perspective.

SIDENOTE

"Make a note whenever you encounter a service or a customer experience that frustrates you, or wish you had a product that met your needs that you can't find anywhere. Then ask yourself, is this a problem I could solve?"

BRIAN SPALY, TRUNK CLUB FOUNDER

PRAISING SHADOWS

I've been into shadows lately. No, I'm not lurking in dark corners. It's just I've become obsessed with shadows after reading *In Praise of Shadows*.

In this tiny book, Jun'ichiro Tanizaki writes, "The beauty of a Japanese room depends on a variation of shadows, heavy shadows against light shadows . . ." And he describes how gemstones, tableware and food items acquire life and richness when seen in "the pale of the shadow."

So I've been noticing shadows. Shadows on pavement. On walls. Furniture. Flowers. Food. The more I notice shadows, the more I notice other things. Simply because I pause to pay attention.

What does this have to do with creativity? Everything. Because the more we notice, the more we make our creative minds "available for seduction," as photographer Sally Mann puts it.

Praise shadows for a couple of days. And see what else you find to praise.

"Find beauty not only in the thing itself but in the pattern of the shadows . . . the light and dark which that thing provides."

—JUN'ICHIRO TANIZAKI, AUTHOR

BROWSE YOUR WAY TO IDEAS

Browsing in Strand bookstore in New York many years ago, I came across *A Technique for Producing Ideas*, by James Webb Young. His little book and concise insights helped articulate a creative flow for me.

That's the power of browsing. "When you search, you find what you were looking for," wrote Leon Wieseltier in *New Republic*. "When you browse, you find what you were not looking for."

Finding what we're not looking for—the magic of serendipity—often becomes the foundation for ideas.

So keep searching. But also take time to browse. Your next idea might be where you least expect it.

SIDENOTE

"Big ideas seem to always come when people are sidetracked, when they are doing something that has nothing to do with their research."

JONATHAN SCHOOLER, PROFESSOR AND RESEARCHER

RESTART TO IGNITE CREATIVITY

What's the first thing most of us do when our laptops and other devices perform poorly? Reboot, of course. Likewise, starting over can be a powerful tool for snags in our creativity. For example:

Restart: Put Aside First Ideas

After his Duke basketball team completes a play—for better or worse—Coach Mike Krzyzewski yells out "Next play!" He doesn't want players lingering on what just happened; he wants them moving ahead.

Ditto with generating ideas. Acknowledge the first idea then put it aside. It's often the same idea others would have in the same situation. That's why some creative people say, "The first is the worst."

Of course, that first idea might also turn out to be the best, and, if so, you can always return to it. But the point is, better ideas than the first one might occur on the "next play." Start with one idea. Then restart with a series of different ideas.

On following pages are two other ways to press the restart button >

Restart: Be A Quick-Change Artist

A quick change by Oscar-winner Jennifer Lawrence early in her career led to her first leading role.

In 2010, Lawrence auditioned in Los Angeles for the role of an Ozark mountain teen in *Winter's Bone*. But the casting director said Lawrence wasn't right for the role because she looked more like an LA starlet than backwoods girl.

Rather than giving up, Lawrence restarted. She jumped on a red-eye flight that night and followed the casting crew to New York, where auditions were continuing the next day. She showed up with rumpled clothes, tousled hair and no makeup. She got the part.

When it looks like all is lost on a creative project, change course with a bold move. Make things happen.

Restart: Take Ideas Elsewhere

Maybe you are trying to cram a round idea into a square hole. Or vice versa. If so, pull back, consider circumstances and redirect.

Chef David Chang first opened Ssäm Bar in New York as an Asian fast food lunch spot. But at the time, Ssäm's location on lower Second Avenue wasn't ideal for lunch crowds.

Chang restarted. Same menu, different hours. By focusing on the 10:30 p.m.–2:30 a.m. business, Ssäm attracted the late-night crowd and, more important, chefs from other restaurants after they left work. This created a buzz in the food community—and a two-star review soon appeared in *The New York Times*, helping Ssäm Bar thrive.

When things go wrong, don't go with them. Restart down a different path.

"Without play, there would be no Picasso. Without play, there is no experimentation. Experimentation is the quest for answers."

PAUL RAND, DESIGN PIONEER

EXPERIMENT

DIAL DOWN DOUBT

"I doubt it."

How many times have you uttered those words? And have doubts and fears prevented you from pursuing ideas? As poet Sylvia Plath wrote, "The worst enemy to creativity is self-doubt."

Of course, having self-doubts is nothing new. "Our doubts are traitors," wrote Shakespeare, "and make us lose the good we oft might win by fearing to attempt."

So what to do about doubt? One thing is to just *do*. Move ahead in spite of doubts. "If you hear a voice within you say you cannot paint, then by all means paint," said Vincent van Gogh, "and that voice will be silenced."

On following pages are three other suggestions to dial down doubt >

"I don't think there is any artist of any value who doesn't doubt what they're doing."

—FRANCIS FORD COPPOLA, FILMMAKER

Dial Down Doubt: Ask Questions

Write down a doubt you're having. Then ask yourself:

- **Is it true?** Is this doubt absolutely true? If not, then why pay attention?
- **Can I handle this?** Do you have the basic skills for this idea or project? If so, why not give it a go?
- **What are the best and worst that can happen?** The best scenario makes risks worthwhile. The worst scenario usually turns out to be far less than feared.

Dial Down Doubt: Nix Negativity

Worry is experiencing failure in advance again and again, according to marketing guru Seth Godin.

And Steven Dubner, coauthor of *Super Freakonomics*, says, "If you don't fill your mental bandwidth with the things most people worry about, you have room to think about more things, ask more questions and create more."

Worry doesn't work, so why let it rent space in your head?

Also, are certain people in your life endlessly spewing negativity? Do they have a problem for every solution? Do they stifle fresh ideas and forward motion?

Friends who aren't friends with our creativity probably aren't truly friends.

Dial Down Doubt: Confirm And Create

On days when I find myself doubting I'll ever write another word—no less an article or book—I read some of my past writings that were well received. Confirmation of creativity! Pretty soon, I'm back at the keyboard, confident that if I've done it before, I can do it again.

To reassure yourself, review your "highlight reel" of winning ideas and projects.

And get to work making something. Writing about Italian fashion designer Elsa Schiaparelli, author Patricia Volk tells of the time Schiaparelli's husband ran off with dancer Isadora Duncan. Alone and penniless, Schiaparelli gave birth to her only child. "And what does she ask for from her hospital bed?" asks Volk. "A lump of clay. She is not happy unless she is making something."

The same is likely true with you. Creative people aren't happy when in doubt and fear—they are much happier when creating.

So dial down doubts by creating something. Anything will do.

SHARE IDEAS

For centuries, childbirth was a major cause of death for women. But in the early 1600s, a British doctor named Peter Chamberlen invented an instrument to assist women in labor.

Dr. Chamberlen and his three sons kept the instrument a secret. When called in to help a mother in obstructed labor, they would make visitors leave the room. And they would cover the mother's lower half with a sheet, so even she couldn't see the instrument.

The device was, of course, the obstetrical forceps. They kept this secret in their family for decades and then sold the idea to another physician, who also kept the forceps under wraps until 1732. For more than a century, thousands of women died during childbirth while Chamberlen and his chosen few sat on the secret.

Your ideas may not be of life-or-death importance, but they're valuable. Don't keep ideas secret—share them. Generously exchange and celebrate ideas.

DIFFERENCES MAKE A DIFFERENCE

An Edward Steed cartoon in *The New Yorker* shows a man behind the counter at an electronic repair shop. On the floor facing the man is a woodpecker. And on the counter is an old TV with holes pecked in the top and sides. The repairman says, *"Have you been trying to fix this yourself?"*

Funny cartoon—and good reminder about creative collaboration.

When facing problems and challenges, we usually try to find solutions using tools we have inside us or in front of us. Sometimes those tools work. And, as with the cartoon's woodpecker, sometimes they don't.

When our tools don't get the job done, we have three choices: We can keep beating our heads against the problem. We can acquire new tools. Or we can seek out people who have different tools.

When we work with people who all look the same, think the same and have the same tools, we come up with the same old solutions. But when we work with people who think differently and have different ideas, we find fresh solutions and new ways to approach old problems.

BEWARE OF NAYSAYERS

Thirty years ago, MIT's Media Lab created a navigation system that it called Back Seat Driver. This was long before drivers began mounting Garmins on dashboards, using cell phone apps or buying factory-installed systems.

But MIT patent lawyers took one look at Back Seat Driver and shook their heads. "They said 'This will never happen, never be done,'" Nicholas Negroponte, founder of Media Lab, told *60 Minutes*. "'The insurance companies won't allow it, so we're not going to patent it.'"

And just like that the naysayers dimmed the lights on a bright idea.

Don't get me wrong—there's a time and place to seriously assess an idea's worthiness. But naysayers don't have time to wait around. They are filled with contempt prior to investigation and already have eyes shut and ears closed.

Ignore naysayers when you can. If you can't detour around them, meet their doubts with determination.

STOP FRETTING AND JUDGING

In the film *Butch Cassidy and the Sundance Kid*, Butch and Sundance are hired as payroll guards for a mining company. In one scene, they head down a mountain to pick up payroll with Percy Garris, the mining company owner.

Butch and Sundance nervously search for bandits hiding behind every bush and tree, even though they haven't even picked up the payroll. A frustrated Garris finally says this:

"Morons. I've got morons on my team. Nobody is going to rob us going down *the mountain. We have got no money going* down *the mountain. When we have got the money, on the way back,* then *you can sweat."*

Garris's words can apply to generating ideas. We block ideas when we agonize over phantom bogeymen—what people will think or whether they will steal the ideas.

Don't worry about that on your way to generating ideas. Focus on being creative. Once you have a payload of ideas, maybe then sweat the small stuff.

Ideas emerge when we don’t allow judgment to block their paths. For today, don’t judge your ideas or those of other people. Don’t judge a single one.

FAST AND SLOW IDEAS

Bob Dylan once asked Leonard Cohen how long it took him to write "Hallelujah." Cohen said it took him three years. Then he asked Dylan how long it took him to write "I and I." And Dylan said, "Fifteen minutes."

Sometimes ideas come slowly, sometimes quickly.

When ideas happen slowly, we need patience and persistence. A visitor arrived at Kaare Klint's studio and asked the Danish furniture designer what he was working on. "I'm working on a chair," said Klint. Eighteen months later, the same person showed up again and asked Klint what he was working on. "I told you," Klint said. "I'm working on a chair."

And when ideas come fast, we need to capture them before they flee. When singer Neil Young gets an idea, he instantly quits whatever he's doing and writes it down. Ideas are a gift, Young told an interviewer, and we aren't being respectful of the gift if we don't pay attention to it.

Sometimes fast, sometimes slow. Take what comes and go with the flow.

"How did it get so late so soon? It's night before it's afternoon. December is here before it's June. My goodness how the time has flewn. How did it get so late so soon?"

—DR. SEUSS, AUTHOR

WHAT NOT TO SAY ABOUT IDEAS

"A new idea is delicate," said adman Charles Brower. "It can be killed by a sneer or a yawn. It can be stabbed to death by a joke or worried to death by a frown on the right person's brow."

Of course, ideas must be examined and critiqued at some point. Critiques help shape existing ideas and spark better ideas. But that comes later, not during an idea's moment of birth.

Watch what you say to yourself and to others when standing at ground zero of idea generation. Wrong words at wrong times bring ideas to a screeching halt.

On following pages are sentences to avoid when generating ideas >

"Hold Ideas Until We're Out Of The Office."

Nothing wrong with heading to a nearby park or coffee shop to generate ideas—a change of scenery often inspires fresh thinking. But if you and your team constantly hold ideas until you leave the premises, you sacrifice spontaneity.

Ideas can bubble up in an instant and vanish just as quickly. Intuition and imagination aren't known for patiently standing in line, waiting for the right time to present themselves.

Carve out collaboration spaces in your facility—areas readily available and easy to access. If you don't have spare rooms, scout out a vacant staircase, hallway or patio. Any place where idea generation can have constant presence in your workspace.

Because ideas have short shelf lives.

"OK, Let's Hear Your Ideas."

That's the call to action often heard at the start of an idea-generating session. Then the usual suspects hold court as everyone else doodles or checks phones.

With most teams, idea generation becomes more potent and participatory if each person spends a few minutes writing down ideas *before* the session shifts into open forum.

Try this at your next idea session: State the problem or opportunity and give people time to jot down their own ideas. For five to 10 silent minutes, let participants furiously scribble or sketch as many rough ideas as possible.

Then everybody shares. *Everybody.* People voice their ideas as someone writes them on a whiteboard. Or, if you like, you can use those ubiquitous Post-It notes. Any method to get ideas out in the open and casually organized.

Now shift into open brainstorming, building off of—sometimes departing from—shared ideas. You'll likely enjoy a more energetic, productive session, with every team member involved in the process.

"Let's Walk Out With One Great Idea."

Bad idea. Generating ideas is releasing; editing is restraining. Telling participants to focus on generating one great idea puts a chokehold on every creative mind in the room.

Here's a better approach: Before idea generation begins, schedule a follow-up session to examine, critique and cull ideas spawned during the brainstorm. Remind participants that final ideas—and maybe that "one great idea"—will emerge in subsequent examining and critiquing sessions, not during the hatching of ideas.

Idea generation is about quantity, not quality. Multiplication, not subtraction. The goal is to walk out with buckets of ideas, not one idea perched on a pillow.

"Don't Waste Our Time With Nonsense."

These words are meant to gain efficiency by reining in farfetched suggestions. But they typically result in a round of safe, humdrum ideas.

Idea generation should be a haven for playfulness, experimentation and generous doses of nonsense. Brainstorming should be stormy. A bit messy. A little chaotic.

"The importance of nonsense hardly can be overstated," wrote Gary Zukav in *The Dancing Wu Li Masters*. "Nonsense is nonsense only when we have not yet found a point of view from which it makes sense."

Encourage wild and crazy ideas. Such nonsense often gives birth to ideas that make perfect sense.

"As Manager, I'll Start Things Off With *My* Idea."

Creative directors or other managers sometimes see this as a way to light fuses for potent idea sessions. But the approach often backfires.

Starting a session this way heads participants in two or three directions. Those easily intimidated will hitch their wagons to the manager's ideas, usually at the expense of their own creativity. Conversely, rebellious participants won't come near the boss's ideas, even though those ideas may have merit. And team members in the middle? They'll likely just sit quietly and let the world turn.

A better approach is for the manager to set the stage by clearly defining the problem or objective—then hold back until later in the session.

"Everybody Keep Your Seats."

These words are rarely spoken but often implied. Participants sink into cushy chairs and remain immobile for the entire session. And energy dissipates.

Participants should feel free to stand up, walk around, sit on the floor, jump up and down.

movement = energy = lively thinking

If I'm conducting an idea session and people start fading, I'll sometimes call for a short break. When participants return, chairs are gone, and everybody stands for the remainder of the session. This on-your-feet overhaul recharges batteries and stimulates idea sharing.

IDEAS HAPPEN AT SPEED OF TRUST

Ideas happen slowly when people distrust their managers. Ideas happen faster when people trust their leaders.

Ideas happen slowly when team members distrust each other. Ideas happen faster when team members trust one another.

Ideas happen slowly when people lack trust that their ideas will get a fair hearing. Ideas happen faster when people have trust that their ideas will be heard.

If you aren't rapidly generating ideas, or if team ideas are slow to arrive, examine levels of trust. Because, as leadership consultant Stephen M. R. Covey says, ideas happen at the speed of trust.

SIDENOTE

"There is one thing which, if removed, will destroy the most powerful government, the most successful business, the most thriving economy, the most influential leadership, the greatest friendship, the strongest character, the deepest love . . . That one thing is trust."

STEPHEN M.R. COVEY, AUTHOR, *THE SPEED OF TRUST*

PERFECTION CAN DO YOU IN

Early. Often. Ugly. When Christa Quarles was Open Table's chief executive officer, those were the words she gave her team after realizing they were trying to perfect ideas before showing them to her.

"No amount of ugly truth scares me," Quarles told *The New York Times*. "It doesn't have to be perfect, because then I can course-correct much, much faster."

Early. Often. Ugly. That's a good mantra when developing creative projects. Early feedback allows easy adjustments and maintains momentum. When focus is on perfection, fear of mistakes and analysis paralysis can overtake creative output.

"As certain as rain will make you wet," wrote Kilian McDonnell, "perfection will do you in."

SIDENOTE

Making a mistake isn’t the problem.

Digging in to defend the mistake is the problem.

MAKE MOST OF MISTAKES

Several years ago, a pastry chef at Osteria Francescana restaurant in Italy adroitly prepared two lemon tarts. But one tart dropped on the kitchen counter and burst open. Chef and owner Massimo Bottura glared at the mess for a few seconds but then shouted, "It's so beautiful!"

Grabbing a clean dish, Bottura created a showpiece by splattering the tart's bright yellow filling across the plate's surface and artfully arranging broken crust.

He then took the other tart, cracked it open and made a second dessert to match. He titled the reinvented dish "Oops! I Dropped the Lemon Tart," and it soon became the restaurant's signature dessert.

Mistakes deserve attention and imagination. With a little creativity, what starts as a mistake often becomes a masterpiece.

GUIDELINES FOR MISTAKES

Making mistakes comes with creativity. But endless mistakes poison productivity. So what's the solution? Selectivity.

Use these guidelines to separate workable mistakes from worrisome ones:

1. **Support only good mistakes.** Good mistakes = strong action, bad results. Bad mistakes = sloppy or lazy efforts, bad results.
2. **Allow only original mistakes.** Have zero tolerance for the same mistake happening more than once. Learning from mistakes and not repeating them is the path to smoother innovation.
3. **Encourage only rescued mistakes.** Mistakes that become disasters will bankrupt patronage and pocketbook. Catch mistakes early and rescue them before they become catastrophes.

SIDENOTE

"I got to sit in on the editorial meeting at The Onion.

"Every Monday, they have to come up with like seventeen or eighteen headlines, and, to do that, they generate six hundred headlines per week. I feel like that's why it's good, because they are wiling to be wrong 583 times to be right seventeen."

IRA GLASS, RADIO PERSONALITY AND PRODUCER

'UNSAFE' IDEAS NEED SAFE HABITATS

Here's a paradox: To generate "unsafe" ideas, people need safe environments.

With "unsafe ideas," I'm not referring to careless ideas, but rather to inspiring, forward-thinking ideas that stretch out of comfort zones.

And with "safe habitats," I'm not suggesting sterile, stale environments but rather workplaces where people feel safe experimenting, voicing opinions and occasionally making mistakes.

Encourage exploration and experimentation. Make sure meetings are designed to stimulate, not bash. Have an atmosphere supported by core principles and solid values.

For groundbreaking ideas, people need grounded environments.

TWO WORDS FOR REGRETS

Do you endlessly kick yourself for mistakes or failures?

In *A Touch of Wonder*, Arthur Gordon tells how a psychiatrist friend of his evaluated patients who were dealing with regrets.

"As long as a patient keeps saying *if only* to me, he's in trouble," the psychiatrist said. "But when he looks me in the eye and says *next time*, I know he's on the way to overcoming his problem."

When you have regrets, especially with your creativity, try replacing "if only" with "next time."

"If only" keeps us planted in the painful past. Swapping that phrase for "next time" heads us toward bright ideas and a brighter future.

SIDENOTE

"The amount of time people waste dwelling on failures rather than putting that energy into another project always amazes me. A setback is never a bad experience. It is a learning curve, an opportunity to grow."

RICHARD BRANSON, BUSINESS MAGNATE

PRIVILEGE OR PROBLEM?

There are two types of people, according to Arthur Gordon, the writer referenced on previous pages. There are those who see life as a privilege and those who see it as a problem.

"The first type is enthusiastic, energetic, resistant to shock, responsive to change," wrote Gordon. "The other type is suspicious, hesitant, withholding, self-centered. To the first group, life is hopeful, exciting. To the second, it's a potential ambush."

People who see life as a problem head out each day looking for the worst in people, places and things. They tend to focus more on problems than solutions.

But people who can view life as a privilege tend to enter each day with a sense of adventure, experimentation and awe—an outlook leading to creative solutions.

If you're stuck, check yourself. Does life look like a problem or privilege?

DON'T GIVE YOURSELF NEGATIVE NAMES

The story goes that when Mahatma Gandhi was studying law in London, a Professor Peters carried a serious grudge against him.

One day Professor Peters returned an exam paper to Gandhi with the word "idiot" scrawled across the bottom. Gandhi approached the professor and said, "Mr. Peters, you signed the paper, but you did not give me a grade."

The story is a good reminder that we don't need to accept negative names others call us. And we certainly shouldn't attach ourselves to any derogatory names we call ourselves. Names like: *"I'm stupid." "I'm a poor speaker." "I'm not creative."*

Pay attention to names you call yourself—the words that follow "I am . . ." See if they are fear-filled and destructive. If so, write them down, undertake any necessary self-improvements and then cast aside those negative labels.

"It ain't what they call you, but what you answer to."

W. C. FIELDS, COMEDIAN

What negative names should I stop answering to?

____

____

____

____

____

____

BOUNDARIES CAN BOLSTER CREATIVITY

I once joined a small group visiting the set of *Saturday Night Live* after Friday rehearsal. Lorne Michaels, SNL's executive producer, emphasized that the show's tight schedule and pressure-cooker pace actually enhance creativity.

"It is axiomatic to me that there's no creativity without boundaries," he said.

Musician and composer Quincy Jones had the benefit of a similar dictum early in his career. His composition teacher, Nadia Boulanger, said to him, "The more boundaries you set, the more freedom you have."

"I didn't want to hear that," Jones told *Smithsonian*, "but she was right."

Coming up are ways to set boundaries to bolster creativity >

Set Boundaries: Limit Technology

If we depend on computers for every answer, we'll often wind up with too many answers. That was the opinion of revered industrial designer Irving Harper, who created the original Herman Miller logo and the first sunburst clocks.

Harper owned an Apple computer, but it usually stayed in his studio closet.

"With a computer, there are too many choices," he told *The New York Times*, and I always like working within limits. If you look at Mozart, who had this strict classical framework—an allegro, an andante, a scherzo, and a finale—you see that within that formula he got results he might never have gotten if he had all the options in the world."

Are you ducking down too many online rabbit holes and overwhelmed with options? Try stepping away from that computer.

Set Boundaries: 'Don't Do' Lists

Determine what you want to do for a project—but also decide what to avoid.

An example of this comes from director Steven Soderbergh. Before filming *Contagion*, he made of list of disaster-movie clichés he wanted to sidestep.

"We had a list we refused to do," he explained to *New York Magazine*. "Can't show the president. No helicopter shots. Can't go somewhere and show people suffering where our characters haven't been. Those restrictions made us think laterally, which was good."

If we know what we don't want to do, it's easier to focus on what we want to do. So make Don't Do lists.

Things I DON'T want to do with a project I'm working on:

Set Boundaries: Cap Resources

We all complain from time to time about not having enough resources. But sometimes too many resources can overload or overburden.

Because of her personal philosophy and practices, fashion designer Stella McCartney does not use leather or fur in her clothing lines. But she embraces those limitations, telling an interviewer, "I like it when I have design restraints."

This mirrors the thinking of creative traffic engineer Henry Barnes, who said he could solve almost any traffic problem with yellow paint and common sense.

If you're stuck or snowed under, try limiting resources. Less can frequently be more when it comes to creative solutions.

Set Boundaries: Creative Time

Determine specific times to move into creative action and stick with schedule.

Isaac Asimov, who wrote hundreds of books, articles and essays, kept to a rigid eight-hours-a-day, four-days-a-week writing schedule.

And author Ann Patchett advises writers to pick a specific length of time to sit at a desk every day. "During that time, you don't have to write, but you must stay at your desk without distractions—no phone, no internet, no books," she says in her essay, *The Getaway Car*. "Sooner or later you will write because you will no longer be able to stand not writing."

This can apply to any creative project. Establish boundaries by setting times to create without distractions. Given time, creativity tends to show up.

Set Boundaries: Personal Deadlines

Deadlines sometimes become lifelines for creativity. Just ask songwriter and singer Jack White.

"Deadlines make you creative," said White in the *Under Great White Northern Lights* documentary. "Telling yourself you have all the time in the world, you have all the money in the world, you have all the colors in the palette, anything you want—that just kills creativity."

We moan and groan about deadlines, but their pressures can demand focus, spark spontaneity and drive delivery. So if you aren't issued deadline, bite the bullet and set deadline boundaries for yourself.

SETTING BOUNDARIES (FOR CREATIVITY'S SAKE)

- **LIMIT TECHNOLOGY**
Step away from screens from time to time.

- **'DON'T DO' LISTS**
For every creative project, make a list of what you don't want to do.

- **CAP RESOURCES**
Self-imposed restraints sometimes help focus creativity.

- **ALLOCATE CREATIVE TIME**
Have specific times for creative thinking and doing.

- **ESTABLISH DEADLINES**
When you aren't given deadlines, set your own.

SIDENOTE

Elegance often occurs when there's nothing left to take away rather than when there's nothing left to add.

Take a project in progress and try reducing or removing elements to arrive at a fresh and better solution.

Save the muscle, trim the fat.

CREATE SOMETHING FOR YOU

Novelist Kurt Vonnegut once wrote a letter to a class of young students, urging each of them to create a six-line poem about anything—but to keep it secret.

He told them that once they completed their poems, they should tear them up and toss them in the trash. "You will find you have already been gloriously rewarded for your poem," he wrote. "You have experienced becoming, learned a lot more about what's inside you, and you have made your soul grow."

This is a meaningful exercise for all of us. Because when we're stuck, it often helps to forget about profits or productivity and create a little something just for ourselves. To see what's inside us. Grow our souls. Be inspired.

What can you create today just for you?

BEST IDEA TOOLS?

Step away from the computer.

Step away from the phone.

Step into a quiet spot with a pad and pen.

Doodle. Draw. Write.

Let the ink flow.

Let your mind go.

Let the ideas grow.

The best idea tools? Pen, paper and imagination.

SIDENOTE

"A blank sheet of paper holds the greatest excitement there is for me—more promising than a silver cloud."

E. B. WHITE, WRITER

STOP DOUBTING, JUST *DO!*

The artist Eva Hesse once wrote her friend and fellow artist Sol LeWitt, saying she had a creative block caused by self-doubt.

Here's a portion of LeWitt's response:

Just stop thinking, worrying, looking over your shoulder, wondering, doubting, fearing, hurting, hoping for some easy way out, struggling, grasping, confusing, itching, scratching, mumbling, bumbling, grumbling, humbling, stumbling, numbling, rambling, gambling, tumbling, scumbling, scrambling, hitching, hatching, bitching, moaning, groaning, honing, boning, horse-shitting, hair-splitting, nit-picking, piss-trickling, nose sticking, ass-gouging, eyeball-poking, finger-pointing, alleyway-sneaking, long waiting, small stepping, evil-eyeing, back-scratching, searching, perching, besmirching, grinding, grinding, grinding away at yourself. Stop it and just DO.

Is today your day to put aside self-doubt and just *DO*?

"Nowhere is there a more idyllic spot, a vacation home more private and peaceful, than in one's own mind, especially when it is furnished in such a way that the merest inward glance induces ease."

MARCUS AURELIUS, ROMAN EMPEROR

EXHALE

GIVE YOURSELF PAUSE

Exhaling and pausing are powerful for creativity. The brain needs time to reflect and recharge.

Pausing is also an important intermission between generating ideas and examining those ideas. Exhaling gives space for the subconscious to spring into action. That's why watching a sunset, strolling a park or taking a shower often produces those "aha" and "eureka" moments.

"Sometimes this happens when you didn't even know you were thinking about the problem," according to Mark Beeman, professor at Northwestern University's cognitive neuroscience program. "It's as if a light turns on and you suddenly see an answer to a problem that had you stumped."

Following are ways to use pausing for more potent creativity >

Pause:
Space Out

There's much ado these days about mindfulness, promoting attentiveness to the present. Without doubt, mindfulness has strong mental and physical values.

However, studies show we hinder creativity if we don't also allow our minds to frequently wander.

"Mind wandering seems to be very useful for planning and creative thought," said Dr. Jonathan Schooler, a researcher at the University of California Santa Barbara, in a CNN interview. "It seems that allowing people an incubation period in which to let their mind wander really helps the creative process."

For creativity, wandering provides wonders.

ACTION

Sit quietly for 15 minutes and let your mind wander. Don't allow yourself to do anything else—no reading, writing, talking and absolutely no digital devices. Don't dwell on work or worries. Just close your eyes or gaze into the distance and let your mind roam free.

Pause:
Hide Out

Open workplaces are the norm—70 percent of offices now have open floor plans. Such spaces can be conducive to interacting and collaborating but disruptive to pausing and pondering.

If you work in an open space, stake out a hideaway—a spot where you can occasionally retreat for a few quiet moments. An empty conference room or unoccupied office. A vacant basement or unused patio. Any secret space to scamper toward when you need to space out.

After I mentioned hideaways during a presentation to an in-house creative group, a designer escorted me to the building's HVAC and electrical room, where he had a folding chair tucked in a back corner. "Don't tell anybody," he whispered, "but here's where I sit and contemplate."

Pause:
Look Up

Next time you're in an airport, coffee shop or other public place, check out people around you. I'll bet at least 75 percent will be looking down at phones or tablets.

Not so many years ago, those same folks might have been gazing or daydreaming. But the gravitational pull of screens now steals time from reflecting and zoning out.

While none of us are willing to abandon devices, we can remind ourselves to look up from time to time. Look up and stare into space. Peer out windows. Study ceilings. (Leonardo da Vinci urged followers to focus on wall stains.)

Or simply put down your phone, close your eyes and take a few deep breaths. Ideas are in flight patterns around our brains, just waiting for clearance to land.

Pause:
Walk Around

Thomas Jefferson, perhaps America's most creative president, was a fan of walking.

"The object of walking is to relax the mind," said Jefferson. "You should not permit yourself even to think when you walk."

Walking provides a path for pausing. It's a healthy way to free the mind, assuming our hands are free of phones and other distractions.

Walking is a "full-body experience," according to author Robert Macfarlane. "Mind and body function inseparably," he says, "such that thought becomes both site-specific and motion-sensitive."

Another persuasive endorsement for walking comes from poet Wallace Stevens, who wrote: "Perhaps the truth depends on a walk around the lake."

Three great places for me to walk:

____

____

____

Pause:
Write Down

Pausing is fruitless if you don't capture what pops up. Keep notebooks handy for fleeting insights and ideas.

"A part of my kind of design and inspiration ethos is that I carry around a leather notebook," said menswear designer John Varvatos. "I sketch in it, doodle in it, write notes in it, put pictures in it."

Writer Dani Shapiro says, "When I sit down with my notebook, when I start scribbling words across the page, I find out what I'm feeling."

As a creative friend says, "Ink it if you think it."

A few notebooks to consider:

- Leuchtturm1917
- Lemome
- Black n' Red
- BooQool
- Moleskine

FIVE WAYS TO PAUSE

- **SPACE OUT**
Sit or walk and let your mind wander.

- **HIDE OUT**
Find some solitude and let go.

- **LOOK UP**
Lift eyes from devices and look around.

- **WALK AROUND**
Take time to take walks.

- **WRITE DOWN**
Capture insights and observations.

QUICK PAUSES

In addition to the pausing suggestions provided on previous pages, there are other ways to take restorative breaks. Here are three:

Climb stairs. When on elevators, we're busy watching the passing floors or shuffling around to make space for people entering and exiting. Instead, hit the stairs as often as possible. Take slow steps and deep breaths. Exercise your body and recharge your brain.

20-20-20 Plan. In his book *When*, Daniel Pink suggests setting your cell phone timer before starting a task. Every 20 minutes, gaze at something about 20 feet away for 20 seconds. This relaxes your eyes and opens idea channels.

Workplace yoga. Stop during the day—especially when you're tired, frustrated or stressed—and do basic yoga stretches right at your desk. Google "office yoga" to find a variety of videos and suggestions.

SIDENOTE

"Elite performers have a common trait: They are all good at taking breaks."

DANIEL PINK, AUTHOR OF *WHEN*

BALANCE DIGITAL LIFE AND REAL LIFE

Filmmaker Tiffany Shlain is a friend of technology—in fact, she created the Webby Awards to recognize outstanding online videos, websites and apps. But Shlain joins the chorus of voices urging frequent breaks from tech devices.

Speaking at a HOW Design Live Conference, Shlain described her family's weekly screen-free day, staying away from TV, internet and emails. They play games, create art, prepare meals and talk. She says it's her favorite day, and her book, *24/6*, explores benefits of turning off screens once a week.

Some communities now designate "unplugged days," encouraging residents to disconnect from devices and reconnect with friends, family and community.

We could all use a round of unplugged days to help balance digital life with actual life. By not being constantly attached to screens, we can more readily connect to real people and real-world observations.

WHEN ENOUGH IS ENOUGH

Knowing when enough is enough doesn't mean to stop reaching for stars. But we can't embrace all stars at once. And some stars we cling to are burning dim. They need releasing so we can reach brighter ones.

Steve Jobs' genius was in knowing when enough was enough. "His sensibility was editorial, not inventive," Malcolm Gladwell said about Jobs in *The New Yorker*. "His gift lay in taking what was in front of him and ruthlessly refining it."

"The gunk" is what Bob Pittman, CEO of iHeartMedia, calls the excess. "With the next 10 things you do, there are two clear winners, two clear losers and six that are gunk," he told *The New York Times*. "So we always talk about weeding the garden."

Is gunk accumulating in your work or life? Recognize when enough is enough and weed the garden.

"A 'Yes' is nothing without the 'No' that gives it boundaries and form."

MICHAEL BUNGAY STANIER, AUTHOR OF *THE COACHING HABIT*

EXAMINE

"Focusing is about saying no."

STEVE JOBS

RECEIVING IDEAS

By now you likely have a firm grip on how to generate ideas. But how skilled are you with receiving ideas from others?

After all, creativity is a team sport.

For every idea tossed out, someone needs to be there to catch it. The NFL's greatest quarterback can't be successful unless he has a receiver to catch his passes. And creative people can't succeed without receivers who listen to ideas, offer encouragement and provide feedback.

Following are ways to make it easy for people to deliver ideas to you >

"There's a widespread belief that if you have solid self-esteem you don't need outside affirmation and praise. This is patently untrue, by the way."

—HARRIET LERNER, PSYCHOLOGIST

Receive Ideas With Cheers

In ancient Polynesian wars, *routis* were cheerleaders for battles. Their job was to inspire the troops by recalling earlier victories and explaining the battle's purpose. Routis joined warriors during conflicts, cheering them on and boosting their courage.

Be a routi for the creativity of others. Explain challenges and opportunities that need to be met with new ideas. Instill confidence by reminding people of their past creative achievements. Build enthusiasm by providing visions of how early ideas could become reality.

People readily share ideas when cheered on during development.

Receive Ideas With Respect

Many years ago, one of my creative directors came to me with a unique product idea. I enthusiastically embraced his concept, eagerly adding my own thoughts and refinements. But the more I talked, the more he slumped in his chair.

When I asked what was wrong, I got an eye-opening answer. "Whenever I present ideas, you immediately start suggesting changes," he said. "This makes me feel like my ideas are never quite good enough for you."

Lesson learned. When receiving a good idea, respect the idea. Avoid additions and alterations. There will be time later to refine and revise. For the moment, let the idea glow, and let its creator bask in glory.

Receive Ideas With Attention

If you are a manager, remember ideas have short shelf lives. If team members feel they must take a number to see you, budding ideas will wither away.

To keep creativity growing and flowing, be physically available to receive ideas. And be mentally available—focused on present moment and open to new directions.

"I don't have an open-door policy, I have an open-mind policy," Mission's CEO Simon Anderson told *The New York Times*. "An open mind helps you hear things, good or bad."

Also, give consistent feedback. If ideas routinely vanish into black holes, people become discouraged. And they soon stop offering up ideas.

"My partner and I have done a lot of research in the area of cognitive science and how it applies to creative problem solving. We know that creative problem solving is not something that an individual can effectively do alone."

WAYNE FISHER, PRESIDENT, ROCKDALE INNOVATION

'TASTE CHEESE' BEFORE CHEWING ON IDEAS

Chef Eric Ripert's Le Bernardin ranks as one of the world's top restaurants.

Before sampling the kitchen's dishes each day, Ripert eats a small piece of Swiss cheese. By daily tasting the exact same type of cheese, he can precisely evaluate his palate. If the cheese tastes extra salty, Ripert knows he's sensitive to salt that day. If it tastes bland, he knows his senses are somewhat numb. By understanding how his palate varies, Ripert can more effectively judge dishes.

Remember Ripert's process when receiving ideas. Chewing on cheese won't help, but you can spot-check your attitude and mindset before accessing ideas.

Take notice of any distractions or prejudices you might be bringing to the critique, such as budget pressures, home issues, whatever. Before hearing ideas and offering feedback, put those concerns aside—or at least be aware of how they might adversely affect your judgment.

WHEN HEARING IDEAS, USE 'THE NOD'

Ever shared an idea with someone who had arms folded and a blank expression? If so, you probably soon lost enthusiasm for your idea, along with any desire to share future ideas with that person.

That's why we need to use "the nod" when receiving ideas. "The nod is when you lean in, and you keep nodding your head when someone is pitching an idea," says business advisor Lisa Gersh. "That way, they get more and more excited about the pitch, and they give you their best work."

As Gersh pointed out to *The New York Times*, smart people often kill an idea by immediately trying to determine what's wrong with it. So she advocates nodding along when listening to ideas.

"It doesn't mean you're going to do the idea," she says. "It just means you're going to listen to the idea and work with the idea."

It takes effort to really listen. To nod. But that's how great ideas begin.

SIDENOTE

Sit down with a team member.
Pop in on a supplier.
Tour a friend's workplace.
Talk with a customer.
Listen to ideas.
Nod.
Just listen and nod.

SHORTSIGHTED BLINDNESS

Many years ago, Sergey Brin and Larry Page offered to sell Google's patent to AltaVista, one of the first search engines. But AltaVista executives said they weren't interested in outside technology.

Yahoo also turned down Brin and Page. Those executives were concerned because Google's search engine would send folks to the most relevant websites. They wanted users to stay on Yahoo.

At that time, Brin and Page were asking $1 million for the patent. Today, Google's monetary value is more than $100 billion.

Shortsightedness can lead to blind spots when looking at forward-thinking ideas. Don't just judge the here and now; also examine the then and there.

And when presenting ideas, help decision makers get past myopia. It's easy for clients to say no to an idea on a table. But if they can visualize your idea's value in the future, they'll have an easier time saying yes.

SIDENOTE

"Nobody believed the Food Network could last . . . I was shortsighted and thought, twenty-four hours of food on TV? They'll run out of things to talk about in four days! But that wasn't true."

BOBBY FLAY, CHEF

SOFT, GOOEY, FAST IDEAS

I heard a nutritionist say that Americans too often head for foods that are soft, gooey and fast. And those foods typically rank low on the nutritional scale.

Hearing her comments, it occurred to me that many unimaginative clients have similar predilections when it comes to ideas.

They want soft ideas. No risks. No rocking the boat. No budgetary revision. No possibility of even slightly upsetting anyone.

They want gooey ideas. Self-serving. Sweet. Innocuous. Overflowing with sugary language and images about their products and organizations.

They want fast ideas. Overnight. Yesterday. No time to explore and experiment, exhale and examine. *"Hey, you're the creative one—give us a brilliant idea while we're sitting here."*

When decision makers crave creative junk food, find ways to change their diet. Soft, gooey and fast is not healthy for their organization or your creativity.

Avoiding Soft, Gooey, Fast

Bosses and clients often demand soft (risk-free), gooey (self-serving) and fast (on-the-spot) ideas. To get around soft, gooey and fast demands, try this:

Soft to solid. Help decision makers understand that strong ideas involve risk-taking. Explain that people have to let go of existing ideas to pick up new ideas. Make it clear you're sensitive to seriously offending people but that energetic, effective ideas involve shaking-up existing mindsets.

Gooey to savory. Discuss how end users see right through saccharine messages. Show a few flowery, self-serving examples from other firms and ask clients if they buy into what they're seeing. They usually get the point.

Fast food to home cooking. Clients often need help understanding what's involved in creating meaningful ideas. Invite them to your workspace. Walk through your workflow. Show a few successful ideas and detail steps necessary to get from initial problem to final solution.

TAKE CONTROL

When Julie Taymor created *The Lion King* for Broadway, she insisted that costumes have authentic glass beads rather than cheap plastic ones.

When the production's financial folks protested that no audience members would be able to tell the difference, Taymor agreed. But then she explained how actors wearing the costumes would know the difference, and that the attention to craft would positively affect performances.

Taymor overcame objections, got the finer beads and the rest is history. *The Lion King* is one of Broadway's longest running plays, grossing more than $1 billon. It took more than glass beads to get there, of course, but the episode is symbolic of Taymor's attention to detail and insistence on high standards.

Decide which details will make big differences in your creative endeavors and stand for their survival. Push for excellence. Take control.

"It's easy to just get comfortably numb, where you're returning phone calls, sending emails, then it's lunchtime, then you have a staff meeting, and another day has gone by. Try to make your day happen. Set positive things in motion in the beginning of your day so it doesn't become just another series of the same thing."

JEREMY ZIMMER, CEO, UNITED TALENT AGENCY

CONSTRUCTIVE (AND CIVIL) CRITIQUES

What's idea-sharing like in your workplace? Friendly, focused and free-flowing? Or do critiques sometimes become a war of words, careening off topic and heading toward carnage?

Sure, an uninhibited wild-west environment can be a plus for creativity, and a level of conflict can "shock us out of sheep-like passivity," according to psychologist John Dewey. But runaway conflict, especially in critiques, can lead to fear, fights and failure.

If your team struggles with presenting and probing ideas, consider a critique method. Every team has different composition and chemistry, so develop a process that works for you.

On following pages is one critique method to consider >

Team Critiques: Steps 1 & 2

As discussed on the previous page, a critiquing method can reduce combat and increase contribution. Methods vary, but on this page and the following two pages is one model to consider.

1. **Tee up.** Presenter lays the groundwork for her or his idea by restating the problem or challenge, along with previously determined goals and objectives. Presenter explains why the idea needs to be considered. This paves the way for Step 2, which deals with what the idea is and how it solves the problem or seizes the opportunity.

2. **Put up.** The presenter now provides a succinct overview of the idea, using the creative brief and other background as foundation. He or she should focus on purpose, audience, aesthetics and attributes, and then on potential issues and obstacles.

Team Critiques: Steps 3 & 4

Steps 1 and 2 on previous page deal with presenter's role for the why, what *and* how *of the idea. The next two steps switch to responsibilities of team members.*

3. **Shut up.** While overviewing the idea, presenter gets to share without questions or comments. Team members remain quiet, avoiding sneers, eye rolls or other body language signaling resistance or rejection. They simply listen attentively, taking notes on questions, concerns and suggestions.

4. **Ask up.** Once presenter completes the overview, questions begin. But only questions—no comments yet. Here's the time to clear up confusion, drill deeper into specifics and move past assumptions. Useful questions often begin with the W's—Why, Who, What, When, Where. Effective answers best begin with "Because . . ."

Team Critiques: Steps 5–7

After questions are answered, it's time for open discussions, evaluations and final thoughts and actions.

Step 5. Open up. The floor opens for comments and conversation. The presenter or team leader sets time limit and helps facilitate discussion. Feedback should be specific and constructive. Avoid personal attacks—focus on the idea, not the presenter. Solutions and suggestions should accompany criticism.

Step 6. Measure up. The group checks the idea against benchmarks not already covered, making sure it meets goals and is consistent with brand.

Step 7. Wrap up. The presenter gathers recommendations. Actions and timelines are determined before adjournment.

Again, this is just one option for critiques. Modify to meet your team and culture. Your goal is a healthy environment where ideas are freely expressed with honesty, clarity and civility.

TEAM CRITIQUES

1. **TEE UP:** *Presenter explains the why of idea.*

2. **PUT UP:** *Presenter gives the what and how of idea.*

3. **SHUT UP:** *Others quietly listen as idea is presented.*

4. **ASK UP:** *Others question presenter on idea.*

5. **OPEN UP:** *Open floor for conversation.*

6. **MEASURE UP:** *Check idea against goals.*

7. **WRAP UP:** *Gather thoughts. next steps, dates.*

"Don't criticize what you can't understand."

—BOB DYLAN, SINGER AND SONGWRITER

SELF-EXAM FOR CREATIVE LIFE

Questions below are adapted from a self-examination suggested by Harry Kraemer, clinical professor of strategy at Kellogg School.

Try asking yourself these questions at end of week:

1. What did I say I was going to do this week?
2. What did I actually do?
3. What am I proud of that I did this week?
4. What am I not proud of?
5. What did I create this week?
6. What did I complain about?
7. How did I inspire others this week?
8. How did I discourage others?
9. If I could replay this week, what would I do?

"The reason many, many people have trouble balancing their lives is that they haven't been self-reflective enough to figure out what they are trying to balance."

Harry Kraemer, author of *Becoming the Best*

"Ideas are only as good as your ability to communicate them."

ADENA FRIEDMAN, CEO OF NASDAQ

EXPRESS

"Telling isn't selling."

BRIAN TRACY, AUTHOR OF *THE PSYCHOLOGY OF SELLING*

CREATIVE PEOPLE GOTTA SELL

Selling doesn't appear on the Favorite Words List of most creative people. We tend to have the baseless notion that ideas should somehow sell themselves and that selling is, well, a bit unseemly.

Truth is, ideas seldom sell themselves. In fact, the better and bolder the ideas, the more they need selling. Because they're different. Risky. Unsettling. Fresh ideas challenge people to let go of old ideas to embrace new ideas. Selling helps that happen.

The selling I'm talking about isn't the high-pressure selling we all hate. That style of selling demands manipulation, because the sales person tries to push something on someone who doesn't need it or can't afford it.

On following pages are reasons to strengthen selling skills >

Selling Skills Boost Spirits

"We've given up on having big ideas because we can't get approvals."

I sometimes hear statements like this when speaking to creative teams. They say it's hard to keep creativity soaring when ideas are nixed day after day.

There's direct correlation between selling success and idea output. High idea-rejection rates eventually result in low creativity levels. But when ideas get thumbs up because they're effectively sold, spirits and creativity soar.

Selling and presentation skills also boost confidence. We're more self-assured when we can clearly explain and present ideas. We enter rooms with aplomb, building trust with our decision makers.

Selling Skills Build Respect

As a creative person, you no doubt want to be a difference maker, not order taker. A contributor, not spectator. That can't happen if nobody's listening.

Learning to communicate ideas and opinions is a game-changer. People notice you. They respect your input. They view you as an adviser.

"The single biggest problem in communications," noted George Bernard Shaw, "is assuming it has taken place." Don't automatically assume others understand your ideas. By acquiring selling skills, you move from bleachers to field. And at presentation time, you're the one they want in the lineup.

Your Ideas Deserve Being Sold!

Your ideas are meaningful. Valuable. Unique. They are different from anyone else's. They are worthy of being seen and heard. Embraced and accepted.

You have an obligation to yourself to effectively present your ideas.

"It's useless to be a creative, original thinker unless you can also sell what you create," said advertising pioneer David Ogilvy. "Management cannot be expected to recognize a good idea unless it's presented to them by a good sales person."

Become a good sales person for your good ideas. Make selling a valuable word in your world.

SIDENOTE

"I like to think of sales as the ability to gracefully persuade, not manipulate, a person or persons into a win-win situation."

BO BENNETT, AUTHOR OF *YEAR TO SUCCESS*

DO THEY REALLY HEAR YOU?

Amsterdam officials rejected conceptual artist Jill Magid's street-art concept to decorate the city's surveillance cameras with rhinestones, saying they didn't work with artists. But Magid didn't give up.

Instead, she returned months later, this time presenting herself as a "security ornamentation professional" at a made-up company. After her carefully crafted presentation, officials gave her permission to bedazzle their street cameras and even paid her to do it, according to *The New Yorker*.

I don't give this example to advocate tricky tactics—such deception is often a sure recipe for ruin. I cite the episode because of what Magid said afterwards: *"I realized the officials could not hear me when I spoke as an artist."*

To connect with decision makers, we need to present ideas in their language, not ours. Know their business. Talk with them, not at them. Otherwise, they can't hear us when we speak.

PAINT PICTURES

Design lets you "rehearse for the future," according to Brian Collins, founder of COLLINS, the brand experience design company.

I hitchhike on his wisdom to suggest that forward-thinking presentations also help decision makers "rehearse for the future." Don't expect people to approve visionary ideas if they can envision only here and now. If your idea focuses on future opportunities, then show decision makers how that future looks.

Help them visualize your idea flourishing in a palpable future. When your idea becomes reality, how will customers respond? How will they feel? Paint pictures. Make it tangible. Make it tantalizing.

And make it optimistic. "Optimism is a strategy for making a better future," said linguist Noam Chomsky. "Because unless you believe that the future can be better, you are unlikely to step up and take responsibility for making it so."

SAY IT LIKE YOU MEAN IT

Someone once asked jazz pianist Thelonious Monk how he was able to get his special sound out of a standard piano. "Well, it can't be any new notes," said Monk. "When you look at the keyboard of a piano, all the notes are there already. But if you *mean* a note enough, it will sound different. You got to pick the notes you really mean!"

Think about that as you prepare to present an idea. What problem does the idea solve or what opportunity does it offer? Write that down. How will your idea look, feel and behave in the real world? Write that down. Why should your client or manager care about the idea? Write that down. What will it take to bring the idea to reality? Write that down.

You've written down lots of words. Learn from Thelonious Monk. Pick the words you really mean. Be sure they'll mean something to decision makers. Then say those words like you mean them.

DO THEY TRUST AND ENJOY YOU?

Zappos, the online shoe retailer, is known for its ability to build relationships with customers. Here's a good example I saw firsthand.

When my wife didn't receive a prepaid label from Zappos to return a pair of shoes, she emailed the company. Here's part of the response she quickly received from a customer service representative:

"My name is Kristina, and I'm the resident coffee expert here at Zappos . . . We are so sorry no label was sent to you quite yet! Not to worry! Thanks to the caffeine I just consumed, I was able to take care of this for you . . ."

This gives a simple formula for building relationships with decision makers.

Understand their problems. Communicate in an honest and human way. Quickly admit mistakes and fix them.

And keep a positive, friendly attitude. Don't be frivolous, but don't be a robotic sad sack. People enjoy and trust people who emit uplifting energy.

SIDENOTE

"When people call our call center, our reps don't have scripts, and they don't try to up-sell. They are just judged on whether they go above and beyond for the customer and really deliver a kind of personal service and emotional connection with our customers."

TONY HSIEH, ZAPPOS FOUNDER

THREE WAYS TO START PRESENTATIONS

"So how's everybody doing today?" That's often a presenter's opening line. It's a lazy way to start.

Get pleasantries out of the way as you first walk in the room. When it's time to present, take control with a strong opening. Here are three easy options:

1. **Story.** Tell a quick human-interest story related to your idea: *"During our research, a customer shared about visiting a competitor's store . . ."*

2. **Question.** Elicit an answer that leads into your idea: *"Our research shows new customers could often use two related services during the first year of doing business with us. What are your thoughts about this opportunity?"*

3. **Quote.** Deliver an insightful quote related to your idea. Better yet, recall words of your decision maker: *"At our retreat, you said, 'If we don't communicate with customers, others will . . .'"*

THEIR PROBLEMS, NOT YOURS

People presenting ideas sometimes eat up the clock bellyaching about how many hours they spent researching markets, developing prototypes, working out kinks.

Cue the violins. Truth is, decision makers are not interested in our pain. They're interested in their pain. They want to know how our ideas will ease their pain. Solve their problems. Make them look good to *their* bosses and customers.

Decision makers accept or reject based on whether they think you understand their problems and whether you have the resources and commitment to solve them, says Trish Bertuzzi, author of *The Sales Development Playbook*.

Forget telling decision makers your problems. Let them know you understand their problems—now and for the future—and that you have compelling ideas to solve those problems.

FEARS OF SNEERS STOP IDEAS

NASA engineers knew they could get a rover to Mars but fretted over how to prevent it from crash-landing on the planet. Eventually, Adam Steltzner and his team came up with the idea of a rocket-powered shell that would hover over Mar's surface while the rover was gently lowered on cables.

When Steltzner shared the idea with others, it was sneered at as "rover on a rope." People said it was crazy. And some probably kept sneering until the day the rover settled on Mars without harm. Then the idea was universally praised as a genius solution.

"Good work and great folly may be indistinguishable at the outset," says Steltzner.

Bold ideas are usually called nonsense until they make sense to the masses. That's why it's important to present ideas, even if you fear they might be called stupid or silly. What they laugh at today may be what they laud tomorrow.

SHAPE BEATS POWER

For eons, most swimming coaches have placed great emphasis on the swimmer's "engine," assuming swimmers with the strongest arms and legs would be the fastest competitors.

But Terry Laughlin, author of *Total Immersion*, focused on "the shape of the vessel, not the power of the engine." He coached swimmers to streamline and balance the body (or "vessel") to efficiently utilize energy.

This "shape of vessel, not power of engine" concept can also apply to presentations. Too often presenters rely solely on "power of engine." With that mindset, extroverted presenters often overdo it, coming across as loud, egotistical and frenetic. And introverted presenters trying to embrace the power mindset—knowing deep down that's not their nature—approach presentations with insecurity and jitters.

On the next page are suggestions for focusing on "shape of vessel" rather than "power of engine" >

Shape Content, Visuals And Delivery

Extroverted and introverted presenters perform better when placing more focus on "shape of vessel" and less on "power of engine" (*see previous page*).

1. **Shape your vessel of content.** Craft content so it flows in a logical order, A leads to B leads to C. Streamline content to be compelling and digestible. Hit the right balance of facts, drama and human interest.
2. **Shape your vessel of visuals.** Carefully edit visuals with a Goldilocks approach—not too many, not too few, just the right amount. Reduce visuals—only a few words or single image. Make sure visuals support messages and don't simply repeat exactly what you are saying.
3. **Shape your vessel of delivery.** Practice. Practice. Practice. Be aware of the strength, tone and pitch of your voice. Give attention to facial expressions and hand gestures. It's not just what you say—it's also how you sound and look as you say it.

SIDENOTE

"Speaking is not an act of extroversion. People think it is. It has nothing to do with extroversion. It's a performance, and many performers are hugely introverted."

MALCOLM GLADWELL, AUTHOR AND SPEAKER

TEASPOONS, NOT BUCKETS

Have you ever wanted to scream while sitting through a never-ending, overwrought presentation?

Sure. We've all been captives of presenters who drenched us with overflowing buckets of enumerations, aberrations and exhortations that left us drowning in a flood of details.

Teaspoons, not buckets. Let those three words remind you to create succinct presentations with an absorbable flow of insights and information, stories and examples. Keep it simple.

On the next two pages are ways to apply "teaspoons, not buckets" >

Teaspoons, Not Buckets, Of Ideas

"Sell the suit, not the buttons." That's an axiom professional sales people use to remind themselves to stay focused on the primary product or big idea, not on small, mundane features that don't really matter.

When preparing presentations for our ideas, it's tempting to cram in every little detail and option we've developed along the way. After all, those mini-ideas cost us blood, sweat and tears.

Avoid the temptation. Instead, strategically determine key ideas and solutions to emphasize, so small stuff doesn't wind up deflating or derailing your presentation. Sell the suit, not the buttons. Teaspoons, not buckets.

Teaspoons, Not Buckets, Of Content

"The simplest way to achieve simplicity is through thoughtful reduction," writes computer scientist John Maeda in *The Laws of Simplicity*.

Try not to fall madly in love with every piece of research. Carefully reduce background information to engaging, illustrative insights supporting your ideas.

And with stories and examples, again remember teaspoons, not buckets. Pack in too many and you'll come across like that undesirable dinner guest who drones on with endless, hackneyed yarns.

"Simplicity is about subtracting the obvious and adding the meaningful," says Maeda. To keep audiences engaged, avoid the obvious in your storehouse of stories. Select relevant examples highlighting major points.

SIDENOTE

Keep it simple ~~is excellent advice for presenters who tend to amplify, augment, digress, detour, expand, exaggerate, overkill and overdo.~~

"Elegance is achieved when all that is superfluous has been discarded."

PAULO COELHO, WRITER

IF TANKING, FINE-TUNE TIMING

Actors and comedians understand the importance of timing in performances. Timing is equally important when presenting ideas. Before your next presentation, consider three time-related factors:

1. **Right time for decision makers.** Just because an idea is ready doesn't mean it's time to present. Before presenting, be sure you understand decision makers. Do you know their wants and needs? Goals and objectives? Likes and dislikes? Fears and concerns? Have you determined an optimum time for the uninterrupted attention of decision makers?

2. **Right time for market.** Is the time right for your idea in the marketplace and for all stakeholders? Or should you hold the idea until conditions change? Do you know all you need to know about marketplaces? Competition? End users?

3. **Right time for resources.** Is timing right for obtaining support to bring the idea to life? Are you ready to convincingly discuss funding? Technology? Human resources? Risks? Rewards? Return on investment?

CONTROLLING PRESENTATION FLOW

"It's about controlling the flow of information—arriving at the right length and the right speed and in the right order," playwright Tom Stoppard told *The New Yorker.* Stoppard was referring to plays, but the principles apply to presentations:

- **Right Length:** Right for the amount of time allocated for the presentation. Right for the idea's scale. Right for the audience. Write out your content. Repeat it aloud. Trim fat, keep muscle.
- **Right Order:** The way you came up with your idea was likely a bit circuitous. Don't deliver it that way. Instead, construct a linear flow that's digestible and enjoyable for the audience.
- **Right Speed:** Deliver too slowly, and you lose energy. Too fast, you lose audience. Practice your pacing. When presenting, watch audience. If people look bored or distracted, speed up. If they seem confused or concerned, slow down.

AVOID HEURISTIC TRAPS

Expert skiers, climbers and surfers sometimes make irrational decisions that cause serious injury or even death. They fall into what's known as a "heuristic trap," where knowledge and experience actually become a detriment, making the athletes overconfident and willing to take deadly risks.

For example, skilled skiers may cause an avalanche by venturing down perilous slopes or accomplished climbers might let themselves get trapped on a mountain in treacherous weather. Past triumphs contribute to ultimate defeat.

Presenters can also fall into heuristic traps. It happens when they know everything about their idea, so they assume they know the best way to present it. Rather than practicing, they "wing it" and suffer the consequences of a disjointed, unfocused presentation.

Don't let experience and knowledge become your heuristic trap. Treat every presentation like it's your first. **The way you practice is the way you perform.**

PRACTICE UNTIL YOU CAN'T GO WRONG

Nick Saban and his University of Alabama football teams have won five national championships. Attending an Alabama practice, I was intrigued by the repetitiveness of the team's drills.

"Everybody thinks you practice something until you get it right," said Saban in a press conference. "You really practice until you can't get it wrong. There's a difference." He pushes his players to practice until they won't make errors in execution, even when facing a variety of teams and circumstances.

This logic applies to prepping for presentations. Rather than just running through a presentation in your head, practice until you can't get it wrong, even when facing changing conditions, tough questions and multiple objections.

No presentation will ever be 100 percent perfect. But repetitive, deliberate practice will polish delivery and keep you from heading in wrong directions, regardless of circumstances.

SIDENOTE

Quickly sign your name on a sheet of paper.

Then drop below the signature and slowly duplicate it.

Not easy when you're thinking too hard about painstakingly writing out your signature.

Same with presentations. If you have to think too much about what to say while in front of your audience, you'll be as shaky and hesitant as that duplicate signature.

Practicing presentations helps you be as confident as you are with your everyday signature.

DON'T BE DOOMED BY THE ROOM

"The room does eighty percent of the work," Jerry Seinfeld told ESPN radio. Great comedy rooms have good sound and focus on the stage.

A room's condition is as significant for presenters as for comedians. Because spaces work for or against presenters, whether it's a boardroom, meeting room or large auditorium.

Most professional speakers—myself included—can rattle off horror stories of rooms gone wrong: flickering lights, noisy HVAC, subpar sound systems, awkward seating arrangements. On and on.

Always preview rooms where you'll be presenting, ideally a day or more before, but at least a few hours in advance. Spend time alone in the space and visualize making the presentation. Note concerns.

On the next page are details to consider during your surveillance >

PRESENTATION ROOM CHECKLIST

Space

- ☐ Sightline problems or other visual obstacles?
- ☐ Window light that might create glare on visuals?
- ☐ Seating arrangements working for or against you?

Sound

- ☐ Does HVAC have annoying noises?
- ☐ Does sound system meet your needs?
- ☐ Could external noises (halls, streets, etc.) interfere?

Stage

- ☐ Is stage sufficient?
- ☐ If no stage, what floor space will you occupy?
- ☐ Could wires or other obstacles cause problems?

If you can correct issues beforehand, go for it. Otherwise, decide how to work around problems—and how to take advantage of room's positive features.

AUDIENCES HEAR WORDS, SEE BODY

A memorable scene in *The Descendants* movie is when George Clooney's character and his daughters sit silently on a couch, passing ice cream back and forth. No word is spoken in the scene, but everything is said.

"The gestures and facial expressions that actors use combine to tell the story visually, along with the dialogue," Alexander Payne, the film's director, told the International Cinematographers Guild.

When presenting ideas, are you aware of your facial expressions, body language and hand gestures? Are those visual elements distracting from your message or enhancing what you're saying?

Pay attention to how speakers and actors you admire effectively use their faces, bodies and hands to benefit communications.

As you practice a presentation, try a delivery while seated. Remain motionless and expressionless as you talk. You'll be quickly reminded of the value added by well-timed gestures and expressions.

CALM JITTERS WITH SELF-TALK

If you get fearful before presentations, talk to yourself. Self-talk isn't a cure-all, but research by the Society for Personality and Social Psychology found self-affirmations help in pressure-filled situations such as public speaking.

"Anytime you have low expectations for your performance, you tend to sink down and meet those low expectations," said researcher Dr. Sonia Kang. "Self-affirmation is a way to neutralize that threat."

What should you tell yourself? I've respectfully revised advice given by the legendary image consultant Dorothy Sarnoff into four affirmations that work well for presenters I coach, as well as for myself:

"I'm excited to speak."
"I appreciate my audience."
"I'm here to help."
"I know what I know."

Read on to learn more about these statements >

Jitters Cure #1:
"I'm excited to speak."

The question typically reverberating through the heads of nervous speakers is, *"What the heck was I thinking when I agreed to do this?"* Sadly, such self-flagellation adds fuel to the fear.

Replace those thoughts with what's known as "anxiety reappraisal." This cognitive-behavior technique basically involves telling yourself *"I am excited"* rather than *"I am nervous."* With this technique, you'll begin transforming nervousness into excitement.

Starting days in advance, tell yourself *"I'm excited to speak."* While making this statement, conjure up gratitude for opportunities to share ideas and insights.

Jitters Cure #2:
"I appreciate my audience."

Too often we think the worst of our audiences, assuming they can't wait to criticize and condemn our every word. Preparing for presentations, we visualize a room full of Darth Vaders and become increasingly afraid.

Fact is, audiences—be they large or small—are almost always on our side. They're rooting for us to succeed, because they want to be informed and entertained by our presentations.

Keep telling yourself, *"I appreciate my audience"* until you truly mean it. Be thankful people are willing to hear what you have to say. And while repeating this affirmation, visualize audience members being delighted by your words.

Jitters Cure #3:
"I'm here to help."

It's easier to share something than to prove something, That's why this jitter-cure statement is gold.

Focus on how you can help. You're not a prosecutor delivering closing arguments in a life-or-death case or head of state seeking approvals to declare war. You're a solution-bearer, a first responder, stepping in to be useful.

Repeating the sentence *"I'm here to help"* when preparing your presentation will positively shape content. And the affirmation shifts your attention away from you and toward your audience.

The word "attention" derives from the Latin *attendere*, meaning "to reach out." As you reach out to others, self-conscious nervousness melts away.

Jitters Cure #4:
"I know what I know."

Making this statement with conviction requires preparation and practice. Preparedness relieves pre-talk pressure, allowing you to confidently glide into your delivery.

In live performances, Beyonce's movements appear effortless because she tirelessly practices. "Part of the reason I rehearse so much is so I can completely let go and relax, she told CBS. "I'm not in my head, and I'm confident."

Know your presentation forward and backward to build confidence and reduce self-consciousness. Then keep affirming, *"I know what I know,"* as a reminder to move out of anxiety and into your audience.

Say It Until You Believe It

From previous pages, you now know four affirmations to calm speaking jitters:

"I'm excited to speak."

"I appreciate my audience."

"I'm here to help."

"I know what I know."

Make them part of your life while preparing for presentations. Repeat the statements days and weeks in advance. Go over them as you practice. Say them in the shower. Replay them before sleep. Review them while traveling to venue.

Repeat affirmations nonstop in those tense minutes just before your presentation. Take a few deep breaths and relax. Then own the room!

SIDENOTE

"For every sale you miss because you're too enthusiastic, you will miss a hundred because you're not enthusiastic enough."

ZIG ZIGLAR, SELLING EXPERT

ROI + RONI = OK

"What's return on investment for this idea?"

There's a question you'll hear sooner or later in any idea presentation. And it's a reasonable one. But ROI inquiries often shut doors on new initiatives, especially when return can't be accurately measured—as is often the case with bold ideas.

That's why idea presenters need to ask decision makers, "What's the RONI—the risk of not investing?"

"Choosing to devote resources to something new may be expensive," wrote Steve McKee, McKee Wallwork + Co. president, in a *SmartBrief* article, "but choosing not to invest has a cost as well."

When presenting ideas, be prepared for ROI questions. If you can quantify return on investment, do so. But ask decision makers to also ponder RONI—what's the risk of *not* investing in your great idea?

HELP THEM DEAL WITH RISKS

While you present ideas, decision makers weigh risks. It's their job. If rewards outweigh risks, chances are good for acceptance. If dangers exceed dividends in the minds of decision makers, say goodbye to your ideas.

When planning pitches, place yourself in the position of nervous decision makers. Step back and view your idea through their eyes. What makes it risky? How can risks be reduced without watering down the idea?

For example, if you anticipate your decision maker thinking, *"This idea is going to suck up weeks of my team's time . . ."* add a risk-reducer like: *"I know this looks overwhelming, but we'll implement in stages and cheaply outsource groundwork . . ."*

Focus on risk-rewards ratios to improve win-lose ratios. Don't weaken ideas to reduce risks. Instead, strengthen presentations.

SIDENOTE

"Every game comes down to two or three plays that have tremendous impact on the outcome."

BILL COWHER, FOOTBALL COACH

Every minute in a presentation is important, but there are critical moments where decision makers will be considering risks and facing doubts. As you prepare, anticipate such moments. Guide decision makers through game-changing junctures.

STORIES SELL

Shopping for dog food, I use reasoning to compare prices and ingredients. But, I admit, those photos of chicken stew or buttered salmon often nab me.

The images create stories in my head about how delighted our dog will be—even though what's in the package looks nothing like what's on the package.

Buying decisions typically involve both reason and emotion. Buyers may assume they use reason alone to determine the value of a product or idea, but emotion tells them *what* to value.

That's important to remember when presenting ideas. If decision makers focus only on reasoning to determine an idea's worth, they'll tend to look only at potential risks. But when you add the emotional pull of stories and examples, decision makers begin focusing on your idea's value in *solving* problems rather than on its risk of *causing* problems.

TELL 'MAN IN A HOLE' STORY

"The primary story told over and over again I call 'Man In A Hole.' Someone gets in trouble and then gets out of it. People never tire of this."
Kurt Vonnegut

When James Dyson first pitched his revolutionary bagless vacuum to retailers, he had a "Man in a Hole" story. He told of cleaning his house with a standard vacuum and being frustrated because the machine quickly lost suction. Looking inside, he found a bag filled with dust and dirt, restricting airflow and weakening suction. Welcome to The Hole.

Dyson then explained how retailers could help their customers climb out of The Hole. With his centrifugal-force vacuum, there's no bag to block air, so the machine never loses suction. Goodbye, Hole.

Create your Man in a Hole story. As Vonnegut said, people never tire of this.

PUNCH AND COUNTERPUNCH

"Everybody's got a game plan until they get hit."
Mike Tyson, boxer

Most of us head into presentations with smart game plans. But our intentions often get KO'd when we're hit with objections.

Prepare for objections with a Punch/Counterpunch worksheet. Draw a vertical line down the center of a page to create two columns. Label the left column "Punch" and the right column "Counterpunch."

In the Punch column, list every imaginable objection. Use as many pages as necessary. In the Counterpunch column, respond to all objections in the Punch column. Don't stop until you're comfortable with every answer.

You probably won't get hit with every objection you've listed. But you'll be ready for whatever haymaker comes your way. And by being prepared, you'll deliver a strong, confident presentation.

Punch	Counterpunch
Objection #1	Response #1
Objection #2	Response #2
Objection #3	Response #3
etc.	etc.
↓	↓

"The fight is won or lost far away from the witnesses, behind the lines, in the gym and out there on the road, well before I dance under the lights."

MUHAMMAD ALI

HOW TO HANDLE OBJECTIONS

You're presenting that shiny new idea to decision makers and sailing toward approvals. But then—uh-oh—here comes a negative comment or strong objection.

How to react? Well, you can get your bloomers in a knot and strike back. Or you can fall into a fetal position and beg for mercy. Or you can respond in ways that save the day, save the idea and actually bolster your relationship with decision makers.

As you know, decision makers don't always fully understand creative ideas. But they are more likely to accept those ideas if they feel fully understood.

Five steps can make decision makers feel understood while helping them better understand details of your solutions:

• Pause • Shift • Acknowledge • Ask • Explain

Following pages explore these steps >

Objection Response 1: Pause

When you get an objection or criticism during your presentation, don't rush to reply. Nod. Perhaps take a sip of water or write a few words in your notepad. Breathe. Smile. These seconds and actions help lower stress and defensiveness.

Your brief pause might also prompt the decision maker to provide clarification or suggestions. That's what happened to Ed Collevecchio, owner of Creative Associates, when a client objected to the voiceover on a video being developed by his firm.

"She said the 'S sounds' were too harsh," says Collevecchio. "My first inclination was to defend the audio, but instead, I paused. And she broke the silence by recommending we try a little audio compression."

That comment let Collevecchio know his client understood sound dynamics. "Turns out we're both musicians, which led to a discussion of mutual interests," he says. "By pausing rather than quickly reacting, the problem was solved, and my connection with the client was strengthened."

Objection Response 2: Shift

As you pause for a few seconds after hearing an objection, begin mentally shifting the objection into a question.

For example, if a decision maker says, *I'm not crazy about the photos you've picked for this project,"* silently shift that in your mind to, *"Will you help me understand why these photos connect with our audience?"*

Or if the client says, *"This idea doesn't match our goals,"* hear him saying, *"Can you help me align your idea with my goals?"*

Shifting negative statements into pleas for help softens the sharp edges of objections. Consequently, you'll likely respond as a supportive adviser rather than defensive diva.

Objection Response 3: Acknowledge

You don't have to agree with an objection, but it's prudent to recognize the objector's concerns. Acknowledge feelings behind the objection, such as: *"I understand why you might feel that way about . . ."* or *"I see how that might be something you would want to consider . . ."*

Lorrie Ross, CEO of Web Marketing Therapy, told me she often uses this technique. "Agreeing with concerns shows you're listening and that you see the decision maker's perspective," she said. "It changes communications from combative to collaborative and opens doors for deeper dialogue."

Understanding is a two-way street. If you want people to understand and embrace your ideas, let them know you understand their wants and needs. Acknowledge their concerns.

Objection Response 4: Ask

To truly understand the decision maker's worries and fears behind an objection, reply with a question: *"Will you tell me more about the problems you see with the photos?"* or *"Can you elaborate on why you think the idea doesn't meet goals?"*

When the objection comes as a "change-that-to-this" directive, Cathy Austin, owner of Loop9 Marketing, finds questions especially helpful.

"By asking the client exactly what they want to convey to the audience with the change, I'll typically receive more specific feedback," she says. "I reply with something like, 'Okay, now that I see what you're trying to accomplish, let us take another look so we can propose the best solution.'"

When dealing with a client who obviously isn't pleased with the presentation but hasn't said why, Austin asks: "Will you tell me what you're thinking?" This usually opens the door for discussions that address real issues.

Objection Response 5: Explain

After acknowledging, probing and listening, you can calmly state your case.

Apply the power of "because" to your reply.

By including "because" in your response, you're more likely to avoid excuses and add explanations. For example: *"I believe this approach will resonate with our audience because . . ."* Or, *"This idea is worth a large portion of our budget because . . ."*

When Lorrie Ross decided to change her consulting firm's name to Web Marketing Therapy, several longtime clients objected, telling her the word "therapy" had too much of a stigma. "I told them I recognized this possible issue, but we were attracted to the new name *because* therapy also means restoring health and soundness," she said.

Of course, if you lack honest answers to objections, don't bluff. Rather than fake it, give a specific time you'll get back with answers.

RESPONDING TO OBJECTIONS

PAUSE

Nod. Sip water. Breathe.

SHIFT

Mentally turn objection into a plea for help.

ACKNOWLEDGE

Let decision maker know you hear the objection.

ASK

Probe for more information about the objection.

EXPLAIN

State your case using the power of "because."

Practice dealing with objections.

While waiting in a grocery line, pick an item in your cart and mentally practice presenting it to prospects. Imagine objections they might have. Practice pausing, shifting, acknowledging, asking, explaining.

You can also practice while stuck in traffic, waiting in airports, sitting in restaurants.

CONTROLLED EXPLOSIONS

Before an article about a person is published in *The New Yorker*, a fact checker calls the person to carefully review exact details.

Revealing this information in advance allows for any "controlled explosion," according to Peter Canby, head of fact checking, giving the person a chance to work through any extreme reactions before the piece hits the streets.

"Controlled explosions" can be useful when preparing to present ideas. If something about your idea may ruffle feathers or cause embarrassment, consider talking beforehand with any decision maker who might be concerned or upset.

Meeting one-on-one, you can manage any controlled explosion in privacy—and hopefully talk through issues—to save your presentation from being derailed by public squabbles or outrage.

"Sometimes you can defuse a difficult situation by simply being willing to understand the other person."

Brian Tracy, sales expert

SIDENOTE

If meeting with someone about a difficult situation, arrange seating so you're next to each other rather than across a table or desk. And if possible, have both of you face a whiteboard showing the problem.

As author Michael Gelb explains in *The Art of Connection*, separating people from problem frees energy for mutual understanding and solutions.

DEALING WITH DISRUPTIONS

It has happened to all of us. The presentation is moving along smoothly, and then—bam! The projector conks out. Or the computer freezes. Or some other disruption distracts our audience and decimates the presentation.

How we deal with interferences can be the difference between a fruitful presentation and a floundering one. We'll never eliminate all distractions, of course, but we can take steps to mitigate their magnitude.

For starters, prepare and practice. The better prepared we are for presentations, the less likely we'll become unhinged when things don't go as planned. Confidence lets us improvise during disturbances.

On following pages are four other tips for dealing with disruptions >

Disruption Defeater 1: Survey Space

Beat disruptions by catching them before they happen. I discussed this earlier (Don't Be Doomed By The Room), but the tip deserves an underscore. By checking the room beforehand, you'll usually detect potential headaches.

Spend time alone in the space. Stop, look and listen. Are interfering noises coming from adjacent rooms, HVAC units or outside traffic?

Are there physical obstructions, sightline issues or glaring lights? Are AV connections, projector and screen ready for business? How's the room's sound and amplification?

Fix as many problems as possible. But even if every issue can't be fully resolved, you won't be caught by surprise. And you'll proceed with confidence.

Disruption Defeater 2: Tell Story

Like most professional speakers, I have a storehouse of stories to fill time if there's a disruption.

If an AV glitch causes delays, I'll sometimes tell of hearing *Saturday Night Live's* Lorne Michaels discuss the show's high energy level. The energy is partly generated by working with a live broadcast, where there's always the possibility of what Michaels called "imminent failure."

I'll connect that little story to the failure of our AV then link it to whatever topic I'm discussing that day. This verbal tap dance effectively fills time until technical problems are solved.

Build your own collection of stories to rely on during emergencies. These can be personal anecdotes, case studies or pertinent examples. Just make sure they are concise, interesting and connected to your core content.

Disruption Defeater 3: Involve Audience

The projector dies during a presentation and what usually happens? The presenter frets with equipment or stands by nervously while audience members tap fingers, pull out phones or, worst case, duck out of the room.

Next time you have a disrupting delay while presenting, you can, as suggested on the previous page, tell a pertinent story. Or instead, have an exchange with the audience.

Come armed with questions to ask in emergency situations. Maybe solicit feedback. For example: *"While we deal with this AV issue, what thoughts do you have based on what I've said so far?"*

Or ask questions that solicit stories. During one lengthy delay, I asked: *"What's the worst problem you've had while giving a presentation?"* This triggered sad and funny tales from audience members.

Don't let audiences tune out during disruptions. Pull them in.

Disruption Defeater 4: Laugh At Yourself

During a major pitch to prestigious decision makers, the laptop with my slides began a high-pitched whine and then went dark. While frantically attempting to resuscitate the computer, I knocked over a water pitcher, soaking my prototypes.

A laugh or cry moment. Against my instincts, I chose laughter. To my surprise, decision makers laughed with me—OK, maybe they were laughing *at* me—but tensions melted. I was able to move ahead, sans slides and prototypes.

Best of all, I was unflustered, and my delivery became more relaxed and personal. Maybe it was a sympathy vote, but in the end I got the decision makers' go-ahead.

When hit with interruptions, take a deep breath, then smile—maybe even laugh—before your next move. If laughter is the best medicine, then laughing at yourself can be a super drug for presentation traumas.

PRESENTATION DISRUPTION DEFEATERS

- **SURVEY SPACE**

  Visit room in advance to uncover potential disruptions.

- **TELL STORY**

  Fill time during disruptions with interesting stories.

- **INVOLVE AUDIENCE**

  Ask questions to engage audience during delays.

- **LAUGH AT YOURSELF**

  Laughing at yourself and the situation relieves tension.

SIDENOTE

"One of the tests of leadership is the ability to recognize a problem before it becomes an emergency."

ARNOLD H. GLASOW,
AUTHOR OF *GLASOW'S GLOOMBUSTERS*

We can't control many things that happen to us, but we can control how we choose to respond.

PREPARE A ONE-PAGE PITCH

You're on your way to deliver a presentation filled with facts and figures, stories and examples, slides and prototypes. But as you walk in, the key decision maker pulls you aside. "We just scheduled an emergency conference call with a major customer," she says. "How about just giving us a fast summary?"

You can ask to reschedule, but sometimes the answer is no. Then what?

Be prepared with a for-your-eyes-only One-Page Pitch—a single sheet you can reference as you quickly overview the idea. No room for fat on the One-Page Pitch—just essentials clearly explaining how your idea solves problems and creates opportunities.

Don't try making the final sale when forced to cut a presentation down to an elevator speech. Use the brief time to convince decision makers your idea is worthy of a complete presentation in coming days.

DON'T FAIL TO FOLLOW UP

It was time for a new roof, so I contacted three firms. One company's salesperson outshined the others. Barry was polished and personable. I agreed to move ahead with his firm, and he promised to email an estimate that night.

But then, no Barry. I called the next morning, and he said the estimate would arrive by noon. A day later, it came. And when I went back with a few questions, it took him two days to respond. Needless to say, we hired another company.

You probably have your own memories of when a salesperson dropped the ball. And you likely took your business elsewhere. Follow-up is a secret ingredient of successful selling. Follow-up builds trust, creates credibility and opens channels for feedback.

Keep reading ahead to find tips on following up >

Follow-Up Tips 1–3: Inform, Inscribe, Involve

1. **Tell decision makers how you'll follow-up.** Before leaving the presentation, provide details of what happens next. If your idea was accepted, discuss action steps for implementation. If the idea was rejected or needs revisions, provide next steps and general time frames.

2. **Make post-meeting notes.** Get alone and get writing. Immediately review the presentation in your mind. Write a short summary. List questions asked, objections raised, insights gained, next steps.

3. **Involve team members.** Hold a download session with team members. Talk about what went right and what went wrong. Discuss reactions and comments of decision makers. Review lessons learned, suggestions for next time and specific action steps.

Follow-Up Tips 4–6: Stop, Salute, Summarize

After completing the first three steps:

4. **Pause before acting.** Before jumping into decisions and actions, give your brain a break—especially if the session didn't meet your expectations. Things appear differently the next day.

5. **Send thank-you messages.** Salute decision makers for giving you their time and attention by reaching out with an email or other appropriate communications. Keep your messages short and sweet, simply thanking decision makers for their involvement and feedback.

6. **Send a summary.** Within 48 hours, provide decision makers with a concise written summary. Include actions, responsibilities and timelines.

PRESENTATION FOLLOW-UP

1. INFORM

Before leaving presentation, review actions and duties.

2. INSCRIBE

Write out what happened in presentation.

3. INVOLVE

Review presentation with team and determine steps.

4. STOP

Pause before jumping into action.

5. SALUTE

Send thank-you messages to decision makers.

6. SUMMARIZE

Provide decision makers with actions, duties, times.

"Great things are done by a series of small things done together."

VINCENT VAN GOGH, ARTIST

4-C CHECKLIST

In *The Checklist Manifesto,* Atul Gawande provides a compelling case for the use of checklists. He explains how simple checklists have helped people succeed, whether flying planes, building skyscrapers or performing surgery.

We sometimes need a strategy that makes up for our inevitable human inadequacies, Gawande argues. "And there is such a strategy," he writes, "though it will seem almost ridiculous in its simplicity . . . it is a checklist."

Once you've prepared your presentation—but before placing your idea's life on the line—step back and scrutinize.

On following pages are four C's to evaluate your presentation >

Presentation Checklist 1: Content

- ☐ Accurate and well-researched
- ☐ Comprehensive, yet focused and concise
- ☐ Recognizes perspectives of decision makers
- ☐ Explains how idea solves problem, now and in future
- ☐ Shows how idea meets needs, interests and goals
- ☐ Demonstrates idea's value to all stakeholders
- ☐ Addresses financial, operational and logistical issues

Presentation Checklist 2: Clarity

- [ ] Avoids backtracks, detours and dead ends
- [ ] Connects with decision makers and their world
- [ ] Avoids jargon that might confuse
- [ ] Clearly explains idea's key components
- [ ] Answers questions decision makers might have
- [ ] Addresses potential objections

Presentation Checklist 3: Creativity

- ☐ Inviting and informative
- ☐ Energetic and compelling
- ☐ Strong opening
- ☐ Strong closing
- ☐ Includes interesting, appropriate stories
- ☐ Includes pertinent examples
- ☐ Plants images about idea's value
- ☐ Helps decision makers see idea in real world

Presentation Checklist 4: Craft

- ☐ Well-organized with logical flow
- ☐ Explicit beginning, middle and end
- ☐ Right length and speed for allocated time
- ☐ Eye-catching, digestible, appropriate visuals
- ☐ Visuals avoid repeating what's being said
- ☐ Professional, proofread printed materials
- ☐ Delivery practiced alone and with others
- ☐ Feedback received from others
- ☐ Adjustments based on feedback

SIDENOTE

"No matter how expert you may be, well-designed checklists can improve outcomes."

STEVEN LEVITT, PROFESSOR AND ECONOMIST

WRAP-UP: 10 TIPS FOR SELLING IDEAS

In this EXPRESS section, we've covered lots of territory on presenting and selling ideas. A good use of time, because ideas collect dust unless we develop skills to sell them.

And the need to acquire selling skills goes beyond formal presentations. Daniel Pink, author of *To Sell Is Human*, commissioned a survey to find out how much time and energy people spend in "non-sales selling"—selling that doesn't involve someone making a purchase.

He found people spend about 40 percent of their time at work involved in non-sales selling—influencing and persuading others in a variety of ways. And those surveyed consider this aspect of their work crucial to success.

As a wrap-up of what we've discussed in this section, ***the following pages provide 10 tips and reminders for boosting selling skills*** >

Selling Tip 1: Make It Their Baby

Decision makers who participate in the creation of ideas are less likely to slay them. That's why David Schimmel, owner of the branding firm And Partners, uses a mantra *of "If they feel they birthed it, they can't kill it."*

To ensure client participation and buy-in, Schimmel aims for client feedback at all stages of the creative process, rather than holding everything for a big reveal on presentation day.

"If you truly collaborate with your clients and let them take credit for ideas," he says, "there's a good chance you'll sell your strongest ideas without having them watered down."

Involve decision makers. Let them see what it takes to develop strong ideas. It's not always easy to include decision makers when developing ideas, but it pays off—especially with final approvals.

Selling Tip 2: See Through Their Eyes

Take a minute to recall your worst college professors. You probably place them in that unfortunate category because they talked over or around you. They came at you from their perspective, not yours.

Remember this when planning an idea presentation. You've worked on the idea for weeks, maybe months. You know it inside and out. But your decision maker's understanding of the idea? Not the same as yours, that's for sure.

Before preparing pitches, ask yourself:

1. *What does decision maker know about the idea?*
2. *What doesn't she know about the idea?*
3. *Why should she care about the idea?*

Answering these questions will help you begin to meet decision makers where they are rather than where you are.

Selling Tip 3: Learn it. Forget it. Play it.

Ill-fated presentations typically go in one of two directions. Either the presenter memorizes and choreographs until the presentation appears stiff and unnatural, or the presenter says, "I know the idea, so I'll just wing it."

The best route lies between these extremes. Consider the approach of jazz great Charlie Parker: learn it, forget it, play it. He would learn and practice a composition until he internalized the piece. Then he would stop fretting over it. This process helped him smoothly perform and improvise before his audience.

Great actors have similar methods. Amy Adams is known for being able to take any sentence written for her and make it sound like she just thought of it.

Strive for focused, relaxed delivery with your next presentation. Learn it. Internalize it. Then relax and present in a conversational style.

Selling Tip 4: Leave Chaos Behind

Generating ideas is often a winding road filled with moments of chaos.

Presenting those ideas, however, should take a straight and narrow path. That's not to say pitches should be dull and didactic. No way. Be passionate and enthusiastic. Be interesting and enticing. Rouse the room.

But don't present ideas the same way you came up with them. That route is filled with doubts, detours and double-backs. Instead, pitch ideas with confidence and with a clear, logical flow.

Make sure your presentation syncs with the decision-making habits of your client. Calm the chaos. Meet decision makers on their mental turf and gently guide them into your world.

Selling Tip 5: Pause Before Starting

I once attended a panel discussion at the Directors Guild in New York featuring Edward Norton and four other actors. The panel quickly fell into a rotation, with each actor commenting on film-related questions asked by the moderator.

When Norton's turn came, he would always pause before giving his answer. Audience members leaned forward, awaiting his words. Norton's responses were no more profound than those of his fellow panelists, but the pauses tended to position him as the group's sage.

With your next presentation, pause before you start. Breathe. Lock eyes with audience members. Capture attention. Build anticipation. Then begin.

Selling Tip 6: Stand Tall, Talk Short

President Abraham Lincoln and orator Edward Everett spoke at the dedication of a cemetery for soldiers killed at Gettysburg. Everett spoke for two hours, delivering 13,500 words. Lincoln spoke for two minutes, delivering 272 words.

Nobody remembers Everett's talk. But Lincoln's Gettysburg Address is celebrated as one of America's finest speeches.

"It wasn't by accident that the Gettysburg Address was so short," said Ernest Hemingway, known for his short, punchy sentences. "The laws of prose writing are as immutable as those of flight, of mathematics, of physics."

In other words, brevity works. When deciding between a longer or shorter presentation, pick shorter. "I wish you had talked longer" are six words you'll seldom hear from decision makers.

HEMINGWAY'S TYPEWRITER AT HIS HOME IN CUBA.

"Poor Faulkner. Does he really think big emotions come from big words? . . . There are older and simpler and better words, and those are the ones I use."

ERNEST HEMINGWAY, WRITER

Selling Tip 7:
Toss Handouts

Handouts are those ubiquitous pages distributed prior to presentations. Presenters envision decision makers patiently following along, diligently in sync with verbal delivery.

But people follow handouts about a well as cats follow tour guides. They'll jump ahead. Hang back. When the presenter is on page one, they're on page six. When the presenter gets to page six, they're back at three.

And pray for mercy if the presenter includes project costs on the last page. That's the first place decision makers look. They'll scan numbers and shake their heads. Then they'll tune out and check their phones.

If you don't want audiences to skip past your ideas, skip handouts.

Selling Tip 8: Bring Leave-Behinds

Leave-behinds are for after the presentation. Decision makers can review them later—hard copy or online—to dive deeper into content.

Leave-behinds provide comprehensive details and also serve another valuable purpose—they can be used to help decision makers sell your ideas to *their* decision makers. No matter how much decision makers may appreciate ideas, they're frequently nervous about how to sell those ideas to *their* bosses.

That's why it's often worthwhile to augment your leave-behinds with photos and prototypes, examples and case studies—anything to help sell your idea.

Before starting your pitch, let decision makers know you'll provide thorough content afterwards. Then watch as they sit back and absorb your presentation.

Selling Tip 9:
Sell With Stories

"'Tell me a story' still comprises four of the most powerful words in English," wrote novelist Pat Conroy, "words that are intimately related to the complexity of history, the origin of language, the continuity of the species, the taproot of our humanity."

Well-told stories are as powerful as facts in presentations because they bring ideas to life. Stories lure in decision makers and transport them toward fulfillment of security, recognition, happiness and other human needs.

"There's something primal about stories," says Lisa Maulhardt of SY Partners. "They help us make sense of our world. By using stories in pitches, we're enticing people to follow along. Stories say, 'Come this way, take that hill, believe in something better.'"

Selling Tip 10: Create Magical Moments

When Steve Jobs first introduced the revolutionary MacBook Air, he walked on stage holding an ordinary manila envelope. When time was right, he slowly slid his new laptop out of the envelope, demonstrating its thinness and lightness. As memorable and dramatic as a rabbit pulled from a hat.

When prospective clients visited pencil-maker Faber-Castell, Anton-Wolfgang von Faber-Castell liked to show the benefits of his pencils. He would often climb a tower and hurl a handful of pencils down to the stone courtyard to demonstrate durability.

When selling ideas, there's no business like show business. Decision makers appreciate facts, but, like all of us, they are drawn to drama. Try adding a touch *of appropriate* drama that showcases and clarifies your idea.

"Obstacles can't stop you. Problems can't stop you. Most of all, other people can't stop you. Only you can stop you."

JEFFREY GITOMER, AUTHOR OF *LITTLE RED BOOK OF SELLING*

DO YOU EXPRESS YOURSELF?

Use tips and tools provided in this book's EXPRESS section to effectively convey your ideas and opinions. To help determine whether you're becoming a powerful, polished presenter, periodically review the following 10 points:

YOU ARE A STRONG, SUCCESSFUL PRESENTER IF:

1. You understand your audience. You take time to know the people and organization. You align content to connect with their wants and needs, problems and concerns, hopes and dreams.

2. You practice. You never wing it. You know content and prepare like a pro. You seek honest feedback. You practice to get it right but also until you can't get it wrong.

3. You check the space in advance. You become familiar with the room prior to your presentation. You work to mitigate distractions and other issues.

4. Your visuals support your verbal content. You keep slides simple and easy to read. You avoid multiple bullet points. Each slide contains only a few words or supporting image.

5. You don't do data dumps. You understand the value of reaching the heart as well as the head. Rather than numbing your audience with nonstop facts and figures, you include vivid examples and related stories.

6. Your presentation flows. You stay focused on the central theme with a beginning, middle and end. You have a linear presentation, moving seamlessly from one point to the next. You work hard to make it look easy.

7. You pace yourself. During the presentation, you stay aware of audience, making sure you're holding attention. You don't speak too fast or too slow. You modulate your voice so it's not monotone and lifeless. You use strategic pauses to emphasize points and to give your audience a momentary mental break.

8. You offer the best version of yourself. You realize each presentation is a performance. You're confident and comfortable with your personal style, but you never phone it in. You bring your best game. You watch body language, posture and delivery, making sure you're not overly casual or unprofessional in the process of being yourself.

9. You engage with your audience. You talk *with* audience members and not *at* them. You project

energy and enthusiasm. You make eye contact. You ask questions and in other ways connect on a personal level.

10. You display commitment. You enter with the mindset of being appreciative of audience members. You are there to help. You understand your presentation is really about selling yourself and the value of your ideas—and that selling is a transmission of enthusiasm and commitment.

MY PRESENTION STRENGTHS:

I NEED TO WORK ON:

YOUR FUTURE STARTS NOW.

Congratulation! You've traveled through this *Creative Zing!* book. You've turned your back on the Zombie Zone and Zigzag Zone and turned toward the Creative Zing Zone. It's now time to move ahead.

Ain't no future in the past. That line from a Vince Gill song has it right—especially when it comes to electric ideas. Creativity lives in today and looks toward the future.

We can learn from the past. We can borrow from the past. We can use past success stories to boost confidence and build credibility. But there's no future wallowing in mistakes or whining about what could have been.

The good news is you can now use the insights of Explore, Experiment, Exhale, Examine, Express to zoom into your Creative Zing Zone.

Imagine the possibilities.

PLAN OR PROCESS?

The factors of Explore • Experiment • Exhale • Examine • Express are presented in this book as a plan for more creative working and creative living.

Do I sometimes suggest clients try the factors as a creative process to generate and develop ideas? Yes—but I always emphasize the 5 E's as *a way*, not *the way*. Because let's be clear: Creativity isn't a mechanical process, and there's no single methodology for generating ideas and solving problems. Creativity can be messy, chaotic and nonlinear. And sometimes it appears to be just good, old-fashioned intuition.

That said, articulated models for creativity have been around since at least 1926, when Graham Wallis outlined his four-stage creative process in *The Art of Thought*. Since then, many individuals and organizations have developed similar methods. And some highly creative people flow through creative steps instinctively, without conscious awareness of applying them.

So if you want to test-drive the five E's as a creative process, have at it. Used as a malleable method, these factors can assist with allocating hours on time-sensitive projects. The factors can also reinforce creative practices during the whirlwinds of deadlines. But never let intuition and flexibility be crushed by an overly rigid process. Without individuality and spontaneity, creativity meets painful death.

READY. SET. GO.

You are now armed with inspiring input for creative output. Here's hoping you'll pick up the tools, techniques and steps to help you become a passionate idea person and powerful presenter of ideas.

The world needs the ideas you can give, so please move into action.

You're ready for your **Creative Zing Zone**—in your work and in your life.

Please keep us posted on your progress!

ACKNOWLEDGMENTS

Some content I first created in other forms for *Fast Company*, *HOW Design* and a few other publications. I've relished working with those publications and am grateful for their confidence in my work.

I'm thankful for all the highly creative people whose thoughts and words are included in this book. Ideas are to be shared, and I'm honored to pass those powerful insights along to you.

To clients, associates and teams I've worked with over the years, thank you for joining me in the **Creative Zing Zone**.

Thanks also to all who participate in my talks, workshops and coaching, as well as graduate-studies students I've taught over the years. I've enjoyed getting to know all of you. And much gratitude for the constant support of family and friends.

And, most of all, to Hope.

END NOTES

14 "The Career Choice," Adam Bryant, *The New York Times*, 9/23/12

17 The Charlie Rose Show, 5/7/08

21 "Whatever We Do Together Will Make Us Different," Zachary Woolfe, *The New York Times Magazine*, 10/7/12

23 "The Bakeoff," Malcolm Gladwell, *The New Yorker*, 9/5/05

28 *A More Beautiful Question*, Warren Berger, Bloomsbury USA, March 2014

34 "Cultivating Creativity," Deb Caletti, *Writer's Digest*, July/August 2015

36 *Chef's Table*, Season 5, Episode 4, Netflix 2018

38 *The Lean Startup*, Eric Ries, Currency, September 2011

42 "How Entrepreneurs Come Up With Great Ideas," *The Wall Street Journal*, 4/29/13

45 "7 Trends To Watch in an Age of Info Overload," Graham Button, *Fast Company*, 10/4/10

47 "Cultivating the Art of Serendipity," Pagan Kennedy, *The New York Times*, 1/3/16

48 "How to Come Up with a Great Idea," *The Wall Street Journal*, 4/29/13

49 *In Praise of Shadows*, Jun'ichiro Tanizaki, Leete's Island Books, 12/77

50 *In Praise of Shadows*, Jun'ichiro Tanizaki, Leete's Island Books, 12/77

51 "Going to Melody," Leon Wieseltier, *The New Republic*, 2/2/12

52 "The Eureka Hunt," Johah Lehrer, *The New Yorker*, 7/28/08

54 *People* magazine, February 2011

55 *The Charlie Rose Show*, PBS, 7/23/08

61 *The Charlie Rose Show*, PBS, 11/12/09
62 "Five Best: A Personal Choice," Patricia Volk, *The Wall Street Journal*, 4/27/13
63 "The Score: How Childbirth Went Industrial," Atul Gawande, *The New Yorker*, 10/9/06
65 "Making Ideas into Reality at MIT's Future Factory," Scott Pelley, *60 Minutes*, 4/22/18
66 *Butch Cassidy and the Sundance Kid*, William Goldman, screenwriter, 1969
68 *Revisionist History* podcast, Malcolm Gladwell, Season 1, Episode 7
68 "Unfinished Business," Geraldine Brooks, *The New Yorker*, 10/17/05
68 *The Charlie Rose Show*, PBS, July 2008
74 *Dancing Wu Li Masters*, Gary Zukav, HarperOne, 10/27/09
78 *The Speed of Trust*, Steven M. R. Covey, Free Press, October 2006
79 "The Advantages of Early, Often, Ugly," Adam Bryant, *The New York Times*, 8/4/16
79 "Perfection, Perfection," a poem by Benedictine monk Kilian McDonnell, St. John's Abbey, Minnesota
81 *Chef's Table*, Season 1, Episode 1, Netflix, 2015
83 "The Wrong Stuff: What it means to make mistakes," by Kathryn Schultz, *Slate*, 6/7/10
85 *A Touch of Wonder*, Arthur Gordon, Jove, September 1986
86 Entrepreneur.com, 10/5/10
87 *A Touch of Wonder*, Arthur Gordon, Jove, September 1986
90 "The Arranger," Lyndon Stambler, *Smithsonian*, March 2008

91 "Undercover Icon," *The New York Times*, 5/2/10
92 "In Conversation: Steven Soderbergh," Mary Kaye Schilling, *New York Magazine*, 2/4/13
93 The Charlie Rose Show, 1/23/15
94 *The Getaway Car*, Ann Patchett, Byliner, Inc., 8/25/11
95 *Under Great White Northern Lights,* The White Stripes, March 2010
98 "How To Grow Your Soul," *Reader's Digest*, 12/16/17
100 Letter from E. B. White to Stanley Hart White, January 1947
101 Letter from Sol LeWitt to Eva Hesse, 1965
104 "The Eureka Hunt," Jonah Lehrer, *The New Yorker*, 7/28/08
105 "Daydream Believer: Is a Wandering Mind a Creative Mind?" Susanne Gargluto, CNN 4/1/15
108 The *Old Ways: A Journey on Foot*, Robert Macfarlane, Penguin, 9/24/13
108 "Notes Toward a Supreme Fiction," poem by Wallace Stevens, 1942
109 "So You Want to Be a Rockstar?" by Kerry Pieri, *Bazaar*, 12/5/13
111 *When*, Daniel Pink, Riverhead Books, 2018
112 *When*, Daniel Pink, Riverhead Books, 2018
113 *24/6*, Tiffany Shlain, Gallery Books, 2019
114 "The Tweaker," Malcolm Gladwell, *The New Yorker*, 11/14/11
114 "Value of Dissent," Adam Bryant, *The New York Times*, 11/16/13
115 *The Coaching Habit*, Michael Bungay Stanier, Box of Crayons Press, 2/29/16
120 "Creating a Culture of Shameless Honesty," Adam Bryant, *The New York Times*, 9/13/13

121 "Individual Innovators Cannot Compete with a Group Going Through the Creative Problem Solving Process," Paul Arnold, *IdeaConnections*, 12/18/15
122 "Eric Ripart—Lessons in Mastery and Mindfulness," *Tim Farriss Show* podcast #268
123 "Treat Meetings Like Improv Sessions," Adam Bryant, *The New York Times*, 6/26/16
125 *Strategic Intuition*, William Duggan, Columbia University Press, October 2007
130 "Know What You Don't Know," Adam Bryant, *The New York Times*, 12/14/13
131 *Human Nature and Conduct*, John Dewey, Modern Library, 1922
137 HarryKraemer.com
139 *The Psychology Of Selling*, Brian Tracy, Thomas Nelson Inc., 2005
144 *Year to Success*, Bo Bennett, eBookit.com, March 2015
145 Body of Work," Alice Gregory, *The New Yorker*, 8/1/16
149 "Tony Hsieh on His Secrets to Success," Robert Reiss, *Forbes*, 7/1/10
151 *The Sales Development Playbook*, Trish Bertuzzi, Moore-Lake, 2016
152 "Crazy Smart: When a Rocker Designs a Mars Lander," NPR, 12/8/03
153 *Total Immersion*, Terry Laughlin, Touchstone, 2004
153 "Terry Laughlin—The Master Who Changed My Life," *Tim Farriss Show*, podcast #276
155 *Quiet Revolution*, the blog of Susan Cain
158 *The Laws of Simplicity*, John Maeda, MIT Press, 8/21/06
161 "Pacing It," Mark Singer, *The New Yorker*, 3/7/11
165 "Jerry Seinfeld, NBA," *The Herd With Colin Cowherd*, ESPN Radio

167 "Home Movies: Alexander Payne, High Plains Auteur," Margaret Talbot, *The New Yorker*, 10/28/13

169 "Self-Affirmations May Calm Jitters, Boost Performance," *Science Daily*, 4/17/15

169 *Never Be Nervous Again*, Dorothy Sarnoff, Ivy Books, 2/28/89

173 *Super Bowl's Greatest Halftime Shows*, CBS, 2/5/16

176 "What's the ROI? Wrong Question," Steve McKee, www.smartbrief.com

178 *The Charlie Rose Show*, PBS 1/28/16

180 *Letters of Note*, Shaun Usher, Chronicle Books, 5/6/14

191 BrianTracy.com

192 *The Art of Connection*, Michael J. Gelb, New World Library, 2017

206 *The Checklist Manifesto*, Atul Gawande, Henry Holt and Company, 2009

212 *To Sell Is Human*, Daniel Pink, Riverhead Books, 2012

223 "The Royal Family Business," Jack Ewing, *The New York Times*, 12/4/13

224 *Little Red Book of Selling*, Jeffrey Gitomer, Bard Press, 2004

228 "No Future in the Past," Vince Gill, *I Still Believe in You*, 1992

ABOUT THE AUTHOR

Sam Harrison is an in-demand speaker and popular author whose mission is to help people expand and express their creativity. He writes and speaks on creativity-related topics and on presentation skills.

Sam draws from experience, having been on all sides of creative communications—agency and freelance, client and corporate, and, most recently, academic, speaking and coaching.

During his years in product development, brand communications and creative services, Sam worked with such clients and associates as the NFL, Major League Baseball, Hallmark, American Express, Merrill Lynch and Hasbro.

The author of three previous books, Sam presents to conferences and companies throughout North America and beyond. He has also taught a variety of classes at Portfolio Center's graduate studies program.

He has been a regular contributor to *Fast Company, HOW Design Magazine*, *IdeaConnections* and many other blogs and publications.

Sam can be found at www.zingzone.com

If you enjoyed *Creative Zing!*, check out these books by Sam Harrison:

IdeaSpotting

How to find your next great idea

IdeaSelling

Successfully pitch your creative ideas to bosses, clients and other decision makers

>>>

If you would like Sam to speak to your group or team on creativity-related topics or presentation skills, visit WWW.ZINGZONE.COM for more information.